Early American Decorative Patterns

AND HOW TO PAINT THEM

BY

ELLEN S. SABINE

DRAWINGS BY THE AUTHOR

COLOR PHOTOGRAPHS
BY HILDA BORCHERDING

BONANZA BOOKS · NEW YORK

Foreword

This book is intended to show how, without previous training or special skill, you can introduce into your home painted decoration in the styles which flourished in the Colonial, Federalist, and other pre-Civil War periods of American history. The techniques explained in the book include country painting, stenciling in bronze powder, wall stenciling, freehand bronze, gold leaf decoration, and reverse painting on glass. In addition to the basic instruction in the foregoing decorating techniques, the book contains a large number of patterns for the further development of skill or for the use of those who are already well versed in the techniques.

ACKNOWLEDGMENTS

It is a pleasure to have this opportunity to thank those who have permitted their designs to be copied into this book, and those who have advised or assisted me in its preparation, namely: Mrs. Hedy Backlin, Dr. and Mrs. Roswell P. Barnes, Mr. James Biddle, Mrs. Julia Borcherding, Miss Hilda Borcherding, Mr. and Mrs. Carstairs Bracey, Mr. and Mrs. George E. Brookens, Mr. and Mrs. Vernon H. Brown, Cooper Union Museum for the Arts of Decoration (New York), Mr. Abbott Lowell Cummings, Miss Mary Aileen Dunne, Mr. Robert Hale, Mr. David Johnson, Mr. and Mrs. George E. Jones, Mr. Bertram K. Little, Mrs. Irene L. Lovett, Mr. and Mrs. Roderick D. MacAlpine, Mrs. John G. McTernan, Metropolitan Museum of Art (New York), Mr. Richard J. Metzger, New York Historical Society, New York Public Library, Mrs. J. Woodhull Overton, Queens Borough Public Library (Jamaica, N.Y.), Miss Gertrude E. Robertson, Mr. William H. W. Sabine, Miss Carolyn Scoon, Mrs. Alden Shuman, Mrs. C. Van Dorn Smith, Society for the Preservation of New England Antiquities, Dr. and Mrs. Louis T. Stevenson, Mr. and Mrs. Arthur Tompkins.

E. S. S.

Contents

[*v*]

PORTFOLIO OF ADDITIONAL PATTERNS

List of Illustrations

LINE PLATES

[*vii*]

BLACK AND WHITE PHOTOGRAPHS

COLOR PLATES

1

Painted Decoration in Early American Homes

Throughout historic time—and indeed during some prehistoric time—men have cultivated arts that transcended the merely useful, and by which they sought to add something to daily life that would render it more interesting and beautiful to contemplate. Painted decoration in the home has been among those arts, and when it is of a kind that conveys to every onlooker a sense of beauty and well-ordered composition, the value of its influence can hardly be overestimated. Its qualities permeate the family, and most importantly and profoundly the children within it. To be surrounded by beautiful things—what better environment could one aim at?

Assuredly, then, we foster a desirable influence when we renew the decorative arts that were practiced by preceding generations. Although not very many examples of painted ornamentation in earlier American homes have survived the passage of time intact, a considerable number of pieces (worn, discolored, thick with grime or with obliterating coats of paint, etc.) have been restored in recent years by the skillful labors of dedicated and enthusiastic researchers. As a result, a large and ever increasing collection of authentic patterns is now available to us as decorative artists in the home.

Earliest Examples

Ornamental painting in America probably started toward the end of the seventeenth century at the mouth of the Connecticut River. The people who originally settled there had been of some substance in England, and with them, or soon after them, came numbers of skilled workmen who met the requirements of their employers not only for

[*1*]

fine homes but for well-made and decorated furniture to go into them. Highboys, chests of drawers, small chests, Bible boxes, and numerous other articles for good living were constructed by capable and industrious artisans. From the district around Guilford and Saybrook came beautiful blanket and clothing chests, painted with colorful designs similar to those found in old English crewel embroideries. At a somewhat later period, Berlin became a noted center for the making and decorating of tinware of all sorts, including coffee and tea pots, tea caddies, trays, canisters, sconces, trinket boxes, document boxes, and boxes for many other uses.

Massachusetts lagged far behind at first, chiefly on account of the Puritans' acquired conviction that ornament, being attractive, must be sinful! But time brought its changes, and this colony also began to turn out decorated chests. Though in general these never equaled the products of Connecticut in quantity or in beauty, mention should be made of the fine chests produced about 1725-1745 in the region of Taunton, decorated usually with graceful vines or tree-of-life motifs. Salem too was noted for its fine furniture makers: much of its furniture was painted in light colors, and delightfully decorated with fruits, flowers, vines, and leaves—an unsophisticated style with an attraction all its own.

Japanning

In this study, we are constantly reminded that early American ornamentation had its roots in Europe and beyond. During the seventeenth, eighteenth, and nineteenth centuries a great deal of Oriental lacquered furniture and smaller pieces was brought to Europe, and in course of time this style of decoration came to be widely imitated there. Thus it was that the craftsmen of Europe developed the art which they called "japanning." They succeeded in imitating the Oriental designs comparatively inexpensively by the substitution of coats of varnish for the lengthy hand polishing employed in the original lacquer work.

The fashionable taste for japanned furniture spread in due course to America, and early in the eighteenth century men trained in this craft were attracted to the more flourishing towns and cities such as Boston, Salem, Newport, New York, and Philadelphia. A wide variety of period furniture, including highboys, secretaries, small tables, clock cases, and mirror frames, owed its ornamentation to local craftsmen.

[2]

Much of their work was very fine indeed; some of it elaborate to a degree.

Pennsylvania "Dutch"

During the middle and latter part of the same century, the German (or so-called "Dutch") decorators in Pennsylvania were painting those beautiful and colorful dower chests that are so treasured by present-day collectors. Theirs was an extension of a folk art that had its roots in Middle Europe, one whose naive charms contrasted strongly with the sophisticated elegance of the elaborate japanned pieces. The German folk artists also decorated chests of drawers, chairs, and all sorts of smaller pieces for use in the home or for its adornment. The outstanding suggestion of this Pennsylvania German work is that of a people who found sheer joy in painting simple straightforward decorations in gay and beautiful colors.

The Sheraton Period

The Revolutionary War brought a temporary eclipse of the ornamental arts, and it was not until the 1790's, when there was a general upturn in American trade, that such arts again began to flourish. This period is known in the history of furniture as the American Sheraton, its chief inspiration coming from the English cabinetmaker of that name. The period is characterized by many pieces of outstanding taste and beauty of line, such as painted settees, sewing tables, dressing tables, mirrors, chests, commodes, and beds. The much admired background colors in light apple greens, grays, pale yellows, vermilion, coral, and white were then in vogue.

It was during this period that painted ornamentation on chairs became the fashion, and every home that could afford it had one or more of the "fancy chairs." The term was rather loosely used to include almost any chair with a painted decoration, and the vogue lasted into the 1840's. The great majority of the chairs were made of inexpensive woods, since mahogany chairs were too expensive for all but a few. Chair manufacturing flourished greatly, especially in the neighborhood of forests from which the wood could be obtained conveniently and cheaply.

Stenciling

But this period of good taste and fine design in decorated furniture did not last long. The small producers began to feel the effect of competition from large factories which were turning out copies of the same chairs and other pieces in bulk. Trying to meet the consequent price-cutting, the small makers and their decorators were led in one way or another to revise their earlier standards. Stenciling in bronze powders—a speedier method of decoration than the purely freehand techniques—was introduced about 1815. Chief among the manufacturers of stenciled chairs was Lambert Hitchcock of western Connecticut, and examples of his work and that of some other early stencilers show exquisite taste and craftsmanship. But, generally speaking, the individual craftsman was in the long run unable to go on competing with factory production. Decorative standards were lowered, work showed evidences of more and more haste and at last the competition and the public's lack of sufficient artistic discrimination put an end for several decades to the production of the painted ornamental design on furniture which is now again so highly esteemed.

Decorated Walls and Floors

The decoration of furniture and utensils was sometimes supplemented in American homes by the decoration of walls and floors, particularly by means of stencils. In Colonial days, well-to-do people could buy fine imported wallpapers from France, England, and the Orient; while wallpaper produced in the Colonies was also available at less cost. Toward the end of the 18th century there was developed a form of decorating walls by painting them so as to resemble wallpaper. This wall decoration, in which stencils came to be most commonly used, was done by traveling decorators who carried their stencil kits and designs from place to place. In the more inaccessible parts of Maine, New Hampshire, Vermont, Massachusetts, and Connecticut one may, if lucky, still find examples of their work, or more likely some small remains of it. Even so, it is often under many layers of wallpaper applied by succeeding generations. In general, the designs used for walls were bright and gay.

Floors too might be painted or stenciled. The commonest pattern was that of a rug with wide running borders and an overall repeated design. The period of decorated floors ranged from the 1780's until well into the nineteenth century.

Beauty in the Home

Even this brief survey may help us to realize how big a part was played by color and design in brightening and enriching the lives of our predecessors in a less mechanized age. They may not have talked or thought much about the reasons for ornamenting their homes in this way, but there is no doubt that they derived great pleasure from these beautiful decorations applied by hand to their home surroundings. Perhaps today we cannot recapture the instinctive folk spirit of those people or the simplicity of much of their life. But even if we must be more conscious and deliberate in our revival of their arts, we still feel the same human needs which they did, and what we create invariably brings us the same satisfying results within and without.

"Decoration" or "Ornamentation"?

The name of the skills we practice is not of great importance to our results; yet in any discussion, written or spoken, terms ought to be the most suitable we can find. It may be noticed that in these pages the words "decoration" and "ornamentation" are used in much the same sense, with a decided preference given to the former. This preference should be explained.

In the early nineteenth century, we find that the term "ornamental artist" was assumed by those rather sophisticated amateurs (that is to say, ladies of leisure) who painted on velvet or glass; modeled in a variety of materials; made artificial fruits and flowers, flower stands, screens, worsted work baskets, and straw baskets; engraved, painted, and beribboned innumerable kinds of boxes from cardboard, glass, and wood; and so on. Thus the word "ornamental" was one of extremely wide scope even with the amateur, while in the professional field it took in inlays of wood, metal, ivory, mother-of-pearl, etc., not to mention the moldings and carvings which characterized the most elaborate productions. In addition, small articles were called "ornamental," not because they were ornamented (sometimes they were plain) but because they themselves were "ornaments," that is, articles added to the more essential furniture with more of an eye to the general effect than to the utility of the additions themselves. In short, the word "ornament" and its derivatives convey at first glance the idea of something raised from the surface, or even of a separate article.

One may conclude, therefore, that in the titling of her monumental book *Early American Decoration* (1940), the late Esther Stevens Brazer made a good choice of the word "decoration," for this word is far less comprehensive than the word "ornamentation," and is most appropriate to the flat, painted, stenciled, and gilded work with which Mrs. Brazer dealt, and with which we are almost exclusively concerned in the present book. At the same time, since the word "ornamentation" does also cover our work, we may vary the language occasionally by using it as a synonym for "decoration."

2
Types of Decoration

The main types of decoration dealt with in this book are freehand bronze, stenciling in bronze powders, gold leaf, country painting, painting on glass, and wall stenciling. With the exception of stenciling, these are all broadly known as freehand methods of decoration. But even in painting "freehand," and when no stencils are used, the designs are first traced on the surface to be decorated; so you have an outline to follow when you begin to paint. Let us see what is involved in each type of decoration.

Freehand Bronze

Freehand bronze is a method of applying metal powders to an underpainting that is partly dry and to which the powder will stick. The technique is centuries old, and in all probability had its origin in the Orient. More than one shade of metal powder was frequently used by the early American decorators, and examples of this are found in conjunction with gold leaf, and sometimes with stenciling. In some cases the painted surface was entirely covered with the metal powder; in others only parts were covered. Delicate shading and beautiful effects can be obtained with bronze powder, and the finished decorations invariably convey an air of elegance.

Stenciling with Bronze Powders

A much quicker method of decoration than freehand bronze employs stencils. The chief period of popularity of stenciling was from about 1820 to 1850, and it was used on chairs, wardrobes, pianos, beds, cornices, chests, and the many small articles used in the home. The early work generally shows the greatest skill and finest detail, being done in pale gold powder, often in conjunction with gold leaf. The cutting of the stencils was admirable, and fruits and leaf veins were delicately shaded. Later, silver was used as well as fire and deeper gold powders. But as time went on, and as competition with factories became keener, stenciling deteriorated, being performed with more haste and less skill. Toward the latter part of the period, many all-in-one stencils were used, and design and execution were equally poor. The chief advantage of stenciling today is that it repeats beautiful decorations for us with a minimum of labor; it does not mean that one must work in a hurry. Besides, stenciling is special fun to do!

Gold Leaf

Gold leaf decoration was used in ancient civilizations and has been adopted and enthusiastically admired wherever it has been introduced. For a combination of magnificence and beauty, nothing can equal it. From the seventeenth century onward, the importation of decorated articles from the Orient spurred first European and then American craftsmen to experiment in copying these superb lacquered wares. Although Western craftsmen seldom equaled the patient Orientals in their extremely fine and detailed work (time was too precious for that), the work they did is justly admired. And if the early high standards declined as time went on, it certainly was no fault of the artists. Once again, the public neglected to give preference to its best artists and craftsmen and began to patronize artistically inferior factory-made products. But no craftsman who once begins work in gold leaf, fails to be fascinated by its enchanting splendor.

Country Painting

This is the name given to that decoration which is specially reminiscent of country folk art: primitive designs, bright colors, and simple forthright arrangements. Subtlety, elegance, and sophistication play no part in this type of decoration. But it is lovely in its kind, at once gay and restful. It is relaxing to do and wonderful to live with; in short, it is a most beneficial antidote to the complexities of our modern mode of living. If in this book only a few country patterns are given, and the emphasis is laid largely on the gold and bronze powder types of decoration, it is not because I love country painting any the less, but simply because my last book, *American Folk Art*, dealt exclusively with that form of decoration, and this time much space must be given to the others.

Painting on Glass

Painting on glass, in reverse, was used to decorate many mirrors and clocks in the old days, and despite the fragility of the foundation, many of these paintings have survived. One also finds a certain number of glass paintings which were made simply to hang on the walls as pictures. The painting work was carried out on the back or underside of the piece of glass, and was done, of course, in reverse. This meant that fine details of drawing and highlights had to be painted first, and background or sky last. Many glasses were done in gold leaf only, or in gold leaf and color; others have stenciled borders or details. Subjects might be almost anything, but great favorites were ships, eagles, and landscapes. Glass paintings are exciting to do, and delightful to look at.

Stenciling on Walls

Wall stenciling was originally done to imitate wallpaper. Most stenciled rooms that have survived appear to belong to the first quarter of the nineteenth century. Simple motifs, symmetrical arrangements, absence of shading, and soft clear flat colors, are their chief characteristics. One finds a variety of forms among the patterns: borders of flowering stems, acorns, and conventionalized leaves outlined windows, mantels, and doors; while deep friezes edged the ceilings. Floral sprays, pineapples, hearts, geometrical designs based on the circle, swags, eagles, and flower-filled urns were popular.

3

Materials Required and Their Care

To do good work in painting and decorating, it is necessary not only to have the proper materials but also to know how to take care of them. The following are the essential required items, with directions for their care.

Paint Brushes. (a) For applying background paints and for varnishing, you can use ordinary one-inch wide flat bristle brushes as sold for a small price in paint stores. The half-inch size is also useful for small areas. Some artists prefer better quality brushes, and find them worth the extra cost. In any case, it is of prime importance to keep your brushes in good shape and perfectly clean.

For cleaning brushes, have on hand a screw-top jar of turpentine, or "brush bath"; this can be used several times over. To clean a brush, first wipe it off on newspaper. Then, after dowsing it up and down in the brush bath, let it stand twenty minutes or more in enough of the fluid to cover the hairs. After this, wash out the brush thoroughly in hot water (not boiling or near boiling), using yellow laundry soap. Rinse well with clean hot water, shake out the surplus water, and shape the brush carefully so that all hairs are in alignment. Stand it up on its handle in a jar where it can dry undisturbed.

Varnish brushes must be thoroughly cleaned each time they are used. In the case of *paint* brushes, however, if you intend to use one the next day, it may be left standing overnight in turpentine or in plain water, so long as there is enough liquid to cover the hairs, and provided the brush is suspended so that it does not rest on the hairs.

(b) For painting the designs you will need the following:

1. Square-tipped ox-hair rigger or showcard brushes. As the size numbers used by different makers are not uniform, the actual size of

the required brush has been illustrated in Figure 1. Buy two for convenience.

2. Square-tipped camel's hair French quill brushes, #0 and #1, also illustrated in actual size in Figure 1. Buy two #1, and one #0. #2 (not illustrated) is useful for larger strokes.

3. Striping brushes. These square-tipped quill brushes, illustrated in Figure 1, are used without a handle.

4. Red sable scroller—a long-haired pointed brush for painting long fine lines and curlicues.

These brushes are cleaned in the same way as described above for varnish and paint brushes, although it is convenient to have a smaller brush bath jar. It is particularly important in the case of these brushes to let them stand in the turpentine, so that the paint and varnish that has worked up into the ferrule is dissolved.

It is only at the end of a painting session that you wash brushes with soap and water (as described above), since you cannot paint properly with a paint and varnish mixture if your brush is still wet from water. So during the painting session, when you want to go from one color to another, just douse the brush up and down in the turpentine, and then wipe the turpentine off with a soft cotton cloth.

It is possible to clean brushes in a dry cleaning fluid instead of in turpentine, but I cannot advise anyone to do so. On the contrary, information has come to my attention which obliges me to issue the emphatic warning that most cleaning fluids that will dissolve varnish are dangerous to health, especially their fumes. Therefore, repeated use of them should be rigidly avoided.

There are, however, one or two jobs that do necessitate use of a dry cleaning fluid, and these are mentioned in the next paragraph, and in the later paragraph headed "Architect's Tracing Linen." Note the warning in the next paragraph.

Trichloroethylene is a dry-cleaning fluid that may be used for making erasures either when painting patterns on frosted acetate or when decorating objects. One small can or bottle is enough as a little on a cloth will do the job. DuPont sells this under the name Dry Clean. Be sure to read the warning on the can. This seems to be the dry cleaning fluid least harmful to health, but even so it should be used only in a well-ventilated room. Use it sparingly and do not inhale the direct fumes. Do not use it to remove paint or varnish spots on your skin. A little, very little turpentine may be used for that purpose, but soap and water is best for your skin.

Tube Colors. *(a)* Japan Colors in tubes: Light Vermilion, Light Chrome Green, and Medium Chrome Yellow. Also Lamp Black or Ivory Black.

(b) Artists' Oil Colors in small tubes: Prussian Blue, Alizarin Crimson, Raw Umber, Burnt Umber, Burnt Sienna, Yellow Ochre, and Yellow Lake (or Indian Yellow). Add a medium-sized tube of Titanium White or Superba White. Note that Prussian Blue, Alizarin Crimson, Yellow Lake, and Indian Yellow differ from the others in that they are transparent colors.

As the name suggests, the Japan colors were originally made in that country, and came to be included in the decorative equipment of, amongst others, our old-time coach painters. Japan colors are opaque, and give a flat, smooth surface. The tubes containing them should be handled carefully because they crack easily, and when this happens the paint soon dries out and is useless. When they are not in use, stand the tubes upside down, with the cap at the bottom. This will cause the oil to rise in the tube and remain mixed with the pigment. A tin can makes quite a good tube holder (see Figure 1).

Keep the caps screwed on all tubes when not in actual use. If a cap sticks, don't try to unscrew it by force and so twist the tube. Just hold the cap for a second or two in the flame of a match, which will cause the metal to expand. Using a cloth to protect your fingers, you can then unscrew it.

If the paint remains inside when you try to squeeze some out, avoid using force, which will split the tube. Probably some dried paint is clogging the opening, and this can be removed with a narrow knife-blade.

Varnish. Buy varnish in the half-pint size. Among the good quality varnishes which I have used are Pratt & Lambert #61 Floor Varnish, Clear Gloss, and E. P. Lynch, Inc.'s Clear Craftseal. I use these as a medium for mixing tube colors in the painting of designs, for stenciling, and also for the finishing coats on a decorated piece. Whenever varnish is mentioned in this book, that is the quality of varnish intended. There are a number of other good quality varnishes on the market which expert decorators have reported to work satisfactorily, among them McCloskey's, Murphy's, and Pierce's. When

[*12*]

buying a varnish, remember that very heavy varnishes are not good for our work.

Never stir varnish. So long as the can has not been opened, the contents will keep perfectly. However, once varnish comes in contact with air, the spirits begin to evaporate; and varnish that shows signs of a definite thickening should not be used. Since there is no way to salvage varnish, proper care should be taken to avoid needless waste. Keep the cover on the can when the varnish is not in use. Be sure the cover is on *tightly*—step on it to make quite sure.

When about one-fourth of the varnish has been used, pour the remainder into small bottles with good screw caps. Fill them to the top. The idea is to expose varnish to as little air as possible. Even when tightly covered, the air inside a partly empty can will thicken the varnish.

Bronze Powders. Pale gold lining, deep gold, aluminum (for silver color) and fire. These powders should be put in small bottles for convenience in handling.

Some of the bronze powders are finer than others, and these are generally called the "lining" powders. The difference is not important at the start of this work, with the exception that the finer or lining powders should always be used in pale gold and in aluminum.

Gold Leaf. One book of mounted pale gold.

Tracing Paper. One roll, thin and very transparent, twenty-one inches wide.

Frosted Acetate. One roll, medium weight. This is a semi-transparent plastic sheet, one side of which is frosted so that it will take paint. Its transparency enables one directly to copy a pattern placed under the acetate sheet, without having first to trace an outline on tracing paper.

Black Drawing Ink.

Crow-quill Pen. A fine-pointed pen.

Drawing Pencils. H, 2H, and 4H.

Decorator's Masking Tape. One roll.

Architect's Tracing Linen. One yard. We make our stencils out of architect's tracing linen, the kind that has a shiny undersurface. This strong fabric will last almost indefinitely if it is properly cared for. It should be kept away from all forms of moisture. Cut stencils should be kept in wax paper envelopes, which can be made from kitchen waxed paper secured with scotch tape. Stencils should be kept lying flat and, immediately after being used, should be cleaned on both sides with dry-cleaning fluid and a soft cloth. They dry in a few minutes. In connection with the use of dry-cleaning fluid, see the caution above (p. 11).

Stencil Scissors. These are cuticle scissors but with *straight* blades. They are obtainable from various sources (one of which is Meilinger & Sons, 913 Eighth Avenue, New York 19, N.Y.) for a few dollars, the price including the special sharpening necessary for our particular kind of stencil cutting. Don't try to cut stencils with an inadequately sharpened pair of scissors. The tiny points must be extremely pointed and perfectly aligned.

Mohair. A piece, about 9 by 12 inches, of this high-piled upholstery fabric, to be used as a "palette" for holding the bronze powders when you stencil or do any freehand bronze shading. Blanket-stitch or overcast the edges of the mohair to prevent fraying. The powders are placed along the lengthwise center fold, as shown in Figure 4. When not in use, the mohair should be folded in half lengthwise, rolled up tightly crosswise and secured with an elastic band. The high pile and the tight rolling keep the powders from mixing.

Velvet. Three-inch wide, silk-backed black velvet ribbon of the best quality (tightest weave) you can get. This is used to apply the bronze powders. Prepare three or four pieces, each four inches long, by sewing the two rough edges together to form a cylinder, leaving both selvage ends open. These are called "velvet fingers." Keep one for freehand bronze, one for gold stenciling, and one for aluminum powder.

Black Paper. For copying stencil patterns, and for practice in stenciling. This may be prepared by painting convenient lengths of ordinary shelf paper with two thin coats of flat black. For directions on thinning black paint, see Chapter 13.

There is a commercial black glazed paper called "Hazenkote Black" (sold by the Hazen Paper Co., Holyoke, Mass.) which can be bought direct in large quantities suitable for groups or teachers. It is also sold in smaller quantities as "black glazed paper" by some of the specialist suppliers who are listed on p. 16.

Primer Paint. Used on all tinware as an undercoat before the background color is applied. A high-grade metal primer paint should be used, one which dries quite smooth and so requires very little sandpapering. It should be stirred thoroughly before use, and may be

[*14*]

thinned with turpentine. Pratt & Lambert Effecto Enamel Primer is good. Also AD Red Sanding Primer. Ordinary red lead is not good enough for our purposes.

Once you have finished using the paint, wipe off any excess paint lying in the rim of the can with a cloth. Then pour a little turpentine on top of the paint in the can, just enough to cover the surface, letting it float there. The turpentine will prevent a skin forming on the surface of the paint. Then replace the can lid and press it down tightly. The next time you open the can, simply mix the turpentine in with the paint, which will probably thin it just enough for use.

Flat Black Paint. For flat black backgrounds, these are currently suitable (manufacturers are apt to change the composition of their brands from time to time):

Sapolin Dull Black Enamel #31, Flat Finish.

Devoe Mirrolac Flat Black.

AD Flat Black.

Among other good makes are Lowe's and Sherwin Williams's.

Paint and Varnish Remover.

Plastic Wood.

Turpentine. One quart. Give the can a shake or two before using.

Steel Wool. #000, or #0000.

Sandpaper. #000 or very fine.

Kitchen Aluminum Foil. One roll. For use in making a "tinsel" picture; and as a palette for mixing colors for wall stenciling.

Crude Oil. Small bottle.

Shellac. This, like the six previous items, is obtainable in the paint stores. Always use fresh shellac. Shellac left over from previous jobs or shellac left standing in half-empty jars for a while should not be used, as it will probably not dry properly, but remain sticky; then your only recourse is to remove it with the paint and varnish remover—a tedious job.

Rusticide. For removing rust. Rusticide is sometimes obtainable from local hardware or paint stores. It is listed in the catalogs of several of our suppliers who are named at the end of this Chapter. It may also be bought, irrespective of quantity, direct from the Rusticide Products Co., 3125 Perkins Avenue, Cleveland 14, Ohio.

Kneaded Erasers. Two or three small ones for use in freehand bronze work. Store in a screw-top jar to keep them from drying out.

Asphaltum. Sherwin-Williams B Asphaltum, and AD Black Asphaltum are makes I have used and can recommend. Masury Asphaltum is well recommended, although I do not happen to have used it myself.

Magnesium Carbonate. 1 oz. cake, usually available at the larger drug stores.

Powdered Pumice. 2 oz. size. Should be bought in a drug store in order to obtain a finer quality than in a hardware store.

Cotton Rags. For wiping up paint or wiping brushes.

Bottle Caps. At every opportunity save bottle caps about one inch in diameter and one-half inch deep—for example, those that come on catsup bottles. Such bottle caps make conveniently-sized receptacles for varnish used in painting designs.

Empty Jars and Bottles. Collect some small jars or bottles, about 2 or 3 inches deep, having good airtight screw tops. These will be needed for holding varnish, turpentine, and cleaning fluid. Bronze powders, which come in packets, are handled more conveniently if they are transferred to small bottles or jars. Cold-cream jars and others of similar types are useful for holding the mixed background colors.

Newspapers. Always have plenty of newspapers on hand. You will need them to spread over your work tables, to wipe brushes, and to use as "palettes" in painting designs.

Where to Buy

General. Many artist supply stores are found throughout the country which carry all or part of the materials used in American antique decoration. However, it is sometimes necessary to go outside one's own locality for particular items, and for your convenience the following list is given of some proven suppliers. Several of these include tinware and woodenware in their catalogs. All will gladly send their catalogs and answer your enquiries.

Arthur Brown, 2 West 46th Street, New York 36, N.Y.

E. P. Lynch, Inc., 92 Weybosset Street, Providence, R.I.

Crafts Manufacturing Co., Massachusetts Avenue, Lunenburg, Mass.

Hoitt & Wentworth, 559 Central Avenue, Dover, N.H.

Brenner's Paint Shop, 8 Samoset Street, Plymouth, Mass.

Block Artist's Materials, 72 Weybosset Street, Providence, R.I.

Empire Artist's Materials, 851 Lexington Avenue, New York 21, N.Y.

Joseph Mayer Co., 5-9 Union Square West, New York 3, N.Y.

The Stone Company, 12 North Street, Danbury, Conn. (no catalog).

[*16*]

Erwin M. Riebe, 149 East 60th Street, New York, N.Y.

Handmade Tinware Reproductions. The following firms have made a speciality in this field.

The Village Tin Shop, 1030 Main Street, Hingham, Mass.

Colonial Handcraft Trays, New Market, Virginia.

Chester P. Galleher, 105 Puritan Road—Rosslyn Farms, Carnegie, Penna.

The Tinker Shop, 142 West Main Street, Milford, Conn. (no catalog).

4

The Painting of Patterns

An important part of your training is the painting of patterns on frosted acetate. Not only does this give you color records of the patterns, but it is a means of getting much valuable practice. There is another important advantage in this saving of your time and energy. Mistakes made in work on frosted acetate can simply be discarded. But a mistake made on furniture means a lot of hard work in cleaning off the surface and repainting the background color—not to mention that inevitable feeling of defeat, irritation, and depression! Nobody wants to waste time or to do unnecessary work.

To paint a pattern, cut a piece of frosted acetate large enough to cover the design you want to do, and attach it to a piece of thin cardboard by three of its corners. Let the frosted side be uppermost, and use small pieces of decorator's tape to fasten the corners. Slip this device into the book so that the acetate will be directly over the design to be painted, and the cardboard under it (see Figure 1). Proceed to paint directly on the acetate, according to the directions which will be given in the succeeding chapters.

Sometimes this method may not be convenient, or even practical, as, for example, where a pattern extends over to another page as in Figures 25, 26. Then it is necessary to make a careful tracing of the complete pattern on tracing paper, using a well-sharpened H or 2H pencil. Mount the complete tracing on a white cardboard by means of small pieces of decorator's tape at the corners. Place the frosted acetate over this. Never anchor your work down to the table surface.

When the pattern has been painted, keep the tracing carefully preserved in your filing folders, as these tracings are necessary when decorating (see Chapter 15, Transferring the Design), and can be used any number of times.

All patterns are painted in stages, and each stage must be allowed to

[18]

dry thoroughly, at least for twenty-four hours, before the painting of the next stage. If you paint on something not thoroughly dry, what is underneath will never fully dry out, and will subsequently cause a cracking off of the paint or varnish covering it.

When painting with French Quill brushes it is important to have pieces of tracing paper on hand, in order to try out brush strokes now and then, and so make sure the brush remains flexible and its hairs in alignment.

It should be borne in mind when painting patterns that all colors are mixed with varnish. We never use turpentine as a medium in painting designs, although we do use it for our background coats of paint. The varnish should be in good condition: don't paint with varnish that has begun to thicken. In mixing color with varnish, be sure it is thoroughly mixed, with no lumps remaining. To "thin" a color in this connection means to add more varnish to the mixture.

Incidentally, the tiny hairlines in Figure 2, Border 1, and the stems in Border 8 are shown as fine pen lines. When painted they will, of course, be slightly thicker, but I have shown them as fine pen lines because the natural tendency is to paint slightly heavier. If I drew a double line to show thickness, you would probably paint the stems still thicker, and so lose the delicacy of the design. This explanation applies to all patterns throughout the book.

Stencil patterns should also be copied for practice, but these are not done usually on frosted acetate, but rather on black paper as described in Chapter 7.

When completed and thoroughly dry, all patterns should be mounted on thin cardboard or heavy mounting paper, and the mount should be, if possible, of the same color as the original piece from which the patterns were taken. The mounting is done by means of small pieces of transparent Scotch tape at the corners. Last of all, the pattern should be given a protective waxed paper flap, folded over at the top and secured by Scotch tape on the back of the mount. Keep patterns standing upright in folders or portfolios, for future reference.

Your first patterns may not be done well enough to satisfy you, but do not throw them away. It is a valuable part of your training and of the development of your critical faculties to look back from time to time at your earlier efforts. And it can be very encouraging too!

5

The Basic Brush Strokes

The foundation of all our decorative painting is the free-hand brush strokes which are shown in Figure 1. These strokes are made with a square-tipped camel's hair French-quill brush. A certain degree of skill in handling this brush and in painting these strokes is needed before you can go on to successfully decorating furniture, etc. To gain this skill one should practice the basic strokes on sheets of tracing paper.

The best kind of table to work at is a rather low one, such as a card table. Cover the top with several layers of newspaper as a protection. Then take a double sheet of newspaper and fold it in eighths for a "palette." We use newspaper for a palette chiefly because it is a kind of paper which readily absorbs superfluous oil in the paint.

Now set out the following necessary items on the table or close at hand:

A tube of Japan Vermilion.

Square-tipped showcard brush for mixing.

Square-tipped camel's hair #1 quill brush for painting.

Tracing paper.

Small jar of turpentine for cleaning brushes.

Cotton paint rags.

Small bottle cap filled with varnish and placed on the palette.

A weight to anchor the palette (a full varnish can will do).

Brush rest—to keep the handles clean (notches cut in a cardboard box cover do well).

Brush Stroke Practice

Place a piece of tracing paper over Figure 1. Squeeze out about an inch of Japan Vermilion on to the newspaper palette. (Squeeze out more as you need it).

Using the showcard brush, dip out several brushfuls of varnish on

[*20*]

to the Vermilion and mix together thoroughly, so that no lumps remain. The mixture should contain enough varnish to be easily manageable yet not so much that it becomes thin and watery and spreads as soon as it has been painted. Lay down the mixing brush on the brush rest.

Take the quill brush and dip it in the red mixture. Draw the brush back and forth a few times on the palette so that the paint works into the full length of the hairs. The brush should be loaded to its full length, not just the tip of it; and each time you go back for more of the mixture in the process of painting, be sure again to load the brush to its full length. However, avoid overloading it: the brush should not be dripping and bulging with paint.

Now hold the brush as shown in the illustration, that is, almost vertically, but slightly inclined toward the hand holding it; the wrist off the ground; and the hand resting lightly on the tip of the little finger. The forearm can rest on the edge of the table. The thumb and forefinger are used to raise or lower the brush as needed—lowering it for a broad stroke, raising it for the narrower parts of the stroke or to finish the stroke.

Paint the broad stripe A in Figure 1, as seen through the tracing paper. Notice how the brush flattens out to a knife-edge when it is lowered to paint the stripe. Now, slowly raising the brush, pull it off to one side, using the knife-edge to end the stroke on a hairline.

Now paint the row of brush strokes B. Begin at the broad end of the stroke by lowering the brush and then gradually raising it to end on a hairline. Hold the brush steady with the thumb and forefinger, without twirling it. The direction and movement of the whole hand and arm are used to arch the stroke. The fingers are used only to raise and lower the brush as needed. Paint each stroke slowly and deliberately. Do several lines of the strokes. Of course, each stroke should be done with one application of the brush—no going back to touch up.

If your strokes end up too thick, you have too much paint mixture on the brush, or you failed to raise the brush enough at the end. Too much paint may also cause the stroke to spread out or "run" after a few minutes. Reload and re-shape the brush for each stroke. With practice, you will learn instinctively to load the brush with the right amount of paint for the size of stroke you want to make. If the brush becomes so flattened that you find yourself painting strokes like the one marked C, turn the brush a little, so that as you lower it, the hairs round themselves for the start of the stroke.

[*21*]

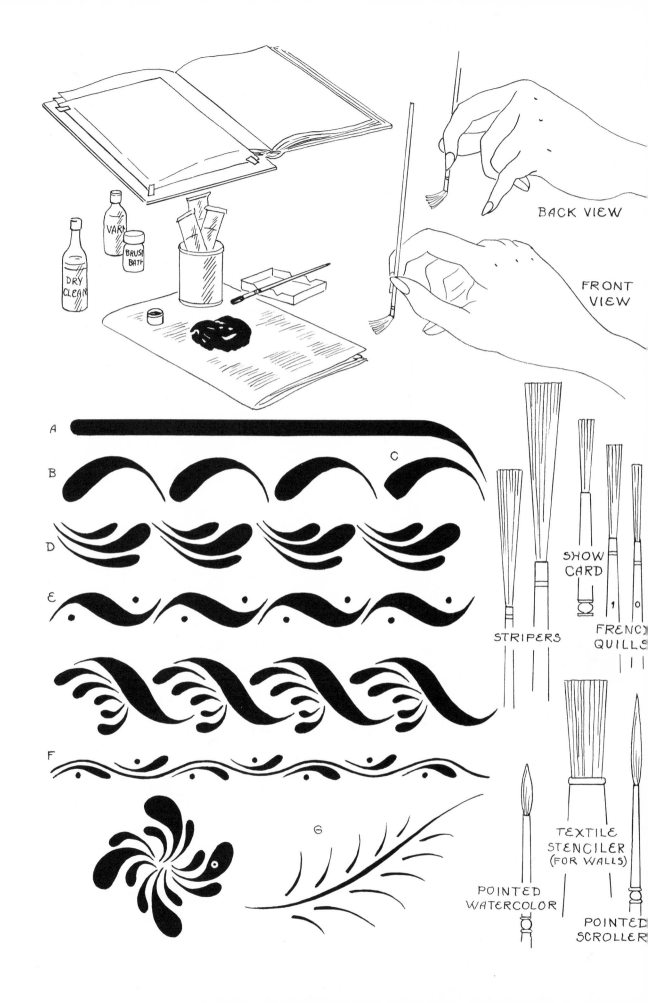

BACK VIEW

FRONT VIEW

VARN

BRUSH BATH

DRY CLEAN

A

B

C

D

E

F

G

STRIPERS

SHOW CARD

FRENCH QUILLS

TEXTILE STENCILER
(FOR WALLS)

POINTED WATERCOLOR

POINTED SCROLLER

To paint the line marked D, turn the book almost completely around, so that you can paint toward you, which is the proper method for this kind of work. In painting a cluster of strokes, start with the largest one each time.

For strokes that begin with a point and end with a point, as in line E, flatten the brush on the palette as you load it. Then, holding the brush high, with the flattened edge pointing in the direction the stroke is to take, begin to paint, gradually lowering the brush to do the broad part, and then gradually raising it again to finish. Go back to the palette again after each stroke to re-load and flatten the brush. Paint all the broad strokes in E first, then the dots.

To paint a dot, round the brush on the palette, and then, holding the brush upright, paint with the end of the hairs. If your brush resists being rounded, paint the dot with one end of the flattened edge.

To paint the thin running line F, flatten the brush on the palette, and paint with the knife-edge. For a vein, as in G, do the same, but lower the brush slightly for the broader parts.

When the paint begins to thicken and you find your brush becoming less flexible, clean both quill and showcard brush by first wiping off excess paint on clean newspaper and then dipping them in the turpentine. Douse them up and down a few times. Wipe off turpentine with a clean rag. Then squeeze out fresh paint on a clean part of the palette, and mix with fresh varnish. Proceed with your painting. It is only at the end of a painting session that you wash the brushes, as described in Chapter 3. Never paint with a water-wet brush if you are using a varnish mixture.

As you paint, keep turning your work around so that it is always at the most convenient angle, one which permits you to draw the brush toward you as you paint each stroke. Keep relaxed. Patience and practice are the keys to success. Practicing half an hour every day for a week or two should give you a fair command of the brush.

For practice you may use Figure 2 as a guide, placing a piece of tracing paper over it. In painting large units, such as those in the top border, we use the same principle of brush stroke, that is, lowering the brush to cover a wider area, and raising it for the narrower parts or to finish off on a point such as the tip of a leaf. We use as few strokes as possible, and we paint deliberately, but at the same time as quickly as possible, so that the finished surface will be smooth and flat. Going over

[*23*]

an area repeatedly with numerous little dabbing brush strokes, will only produce a rumpled, messy, and amateurish surface.

In the top border, Leaf A has been marked off into four areas, each one representing a brush stroke. Paint the strokes in their numerical order, each stroke slightly overlapping the previous one, so that you leave no spaces unpainted to which you have to go back for touching up. Never paint such a unit by outlining it first with the paint brush and then filling in; this type of work will inevitably show up on the finished surface and proclaim your lack of mastery. Flower B is similarly marked off in areas, and should be painted in four strokes, as numbered.

For the time being, disregard all superimposed details in Borders 1, 5, and 8, which are explained in the chapter on Freehand Bronze. In Border 2, paint the running line first, as a guide line, then the brush strokes, and lastly the dots. All the borders are freehand bronze or gold leaf borders, techniques which are described in subsequent chapters.

6

Freehand Bronze

Freehand bronze painting is the description given to a method of applying bronze powders to a painted surface that is still only partly dry. The word "bronze" in this connection means all the metal powders which give the effect not only of bronze but of silver, gold, copper, and brass in a great variety of shades. Note that we do *not* paint with a liquid metal paint: we use these metal powders dry.

In order that the loose powder may not stick where it is not wanted, we must start with an absolutely dry background of flat or dull paint. The pattern is then painted on the background with a mixture of Japan paint and varnish. The result is allowed to dry to a certain tacky stage, whereupon the metal powders are applied with a piece of velvet, either completely covering the tacky surfare, as shown in Illustration 7, Black penline or painted details are added at a later stage.
or partially covering it in a shaded manner as shown in Color Plate II.

To Copy a Border Pattern

1. Turn to the gold leaf patterns in Figure 2. These will serve excellently for our first freehand bronze practice. Cut a piece of frosted acetate large enough to cover the upper half of the page, and attach it, frosted side up, by three of its corners to a thin cardboard. Use small bits of masking tape. Slip this over the page and into the book as shown in Figure 1, so that the acetate is just over the upper half of Figure 2. Using the illustrations under the acetate as a guide, you will paint directly on the acetate. Review the chapter on Basic Brush Strokes.

2. In one corner of your newspaper palette place a small mound of pale gold lining powder. Set out a "velvet finger." Now, on the palette mix some Japan Vermilion and varnish together as described in Chapter 5, but this time using enough varnish to make the mixture rather thin—

A   B   1. ICE BUCKET

2 SMALL BOX

3 CHEST OF DRAWERS

4 BOX

5 BELLOWS

6 LACE EDGE TRAY

7 HIGHBOY

8 TRAY

so thin that when painted on the acetate it will be a slightly transparent light red.

Using a #1 quill brush, and disregarding all superimposed details, start with Border 1 by painting first the larger leaves and flowers, then the smaller leaves, and last of all the tiny hairlines. Be sure not to overload the brush. Apply the mixture evenly, without leaving any overly wet places. Paint carefully, so that you do not have to go back to touch up any places. Paint it and leave it. Your work should have a smooth glossy surface.

In working along, keep watch on the parts already painted, and as they begin to dry, but before they are actually dry, apply the pale gold powder with a "velvet finger." (Figure 4 shows you how to wrap the velvet tightly around your forefinger). Pick up a good supply of gold powder on the fingertip, and use a small circular motion and a very light touch to apply it. Do not dab it on. Just skim the surface lightly with the small circular motion. Continue painting and applying the powder to the drying areas.

The trick is to apply the powder at just the right stage of tackiness. If you do it too soon, or use the velvet with too much pressure, some of the hairs of the velvet may stick to the surface, or the surface may be roughened. If you wait too long, the surface will be too dry for the powder to stick. Practice will give you the proper timing. Remember that on a dry day the surface will dry more quickly than on a wet day.

In painting a pattern, or a particular section of a pattern, we usually paint the larger parts first, then the medium-sized ones, and so on down to the smallest. This is done because the larger areas take longer to dry, whereas the tiny hairlines dry almost at once.

When you have finished applying the last of the gold powder, lay the pattern aside to dry for twenty-four hours.

3. Wipe off the excess loose gold powder with a soft cloth. If the powder sticks to the acetate, use a damp sponge, patting the surface dry with a clean linen towel. Be sure to remove every bit of loose powder on the pattern and on the acetate.

A "kneaded rubber" eraser is sometimes useful at this stage in removing excess powder from the acetate. Cut a fresh eraser in half; take the half you intend to use and pull it apart into small pieces; then knead the pieces back together again, using the fingers of one hand to knead the material in the palm of the other. The warmth of the hands will help, and you will find that you can form the eraser into any desired

[27]

FIGURE 2   GOLD LEAF BORDERS

shape, pulling it out to a point if you like. With this eraser, go over the acetate, and it will pick up the excess powder. Be careful not to touch the painted design. From time to time, re-knead the rubber to get a clean surface on it.

With a crow quill pen and black drawing ink, draw in the details of veins, stamens, etc., shown in white on Figure 2. Allow an hour for the ink to harden.

For practice do the rest of the borders in Figure 2, and the patterns in Figures 21-23, 25-27, and 29.

Excess Bronze Powder

In decorating a painted object, it is sometimes difficult to wipe off the excess loose powder after the twenty-four-hour drying period. A metal object may be held under running cold water. For a wooden object, use a damp sponge, patting the surface dry afterwards. If powder still sticks, use the kneaded eraser, as described above. There are, however, two things you can do before the decoration is applied to diminish this hazard: (a) Wait one month after the last coat of background paint has been applied, to allow the paint to harden. A longer wait is still better. (b) Just before you transfer the pattern outlines (see Chapter 15), take a *pinch* of whiting powder, and, with your finger tips, rub it lightly over the painted surface. Blow off all excess powder.

The fine bronze lining powders tend to stick where they are not wanted, but as they give a more beautiful surface than the coarser powders, it is worth while to learn how to use them. A little patience and practice will get results.

The Protective Coat of Varnish

Understandably enough, beginners are often a bit shaky when they first come to draw the pen and ink lines and details on the gold surface. They may make mistakes which they find difficult to rectify.

One way to cope with this problem is to give the gold surface a coat of varnish (see p. 35). Wait twenty-four hours, and then go over the varnish lightly with #000 steel wool, applying just enough pressure to take off the gloss, which disappears almost at once. Dust off the surface and then transfer (see p. 85) a few of the main lines of the pen and ink detail, to act as a broad guide. But leave most of the detail to be done by eye, thus preserving that freedom and spontaneity which is the charm of patterns of this type.

Warning

There is a warning, however, which must be heeded whenever you use a protective coat of varnish over bronze powders during the decoration of a piece of furniture or any other object. The decoration must be completed as soon as possible and the finishing coats of varnish applied without delay; otherwise the metal powder will probably tarnish. I have seen gold powder that has had one or two coats of varnish become tarnished within six weeks. Why this should happen I don't know. But if the six or more finishing coats of varnish are applied without any lapse of time, the beautiful gold powder surface is perfectly safe.

Shaded Freehand Bronze

Another type of freehand bronze decoration is shown in Color Plate II. Instead of the entire painted surface being covered with bronze powder, here the powder is applied with shaded effects, and a good deal of the underpainting (black and green in this case) is left exposed to form part of the decoration.

This kind of decoration is somewhat more advanced, and so the patterns for it are given later in the book (Figures 56 and 57). The beginner will use them after some more practice in painting.

7

Stenciling in Bronze Powders

Stenciling is a technique which many amateurs tend to regard disdainfully, as a form of decoration not worthy of their serious study. They may have at some time come upon crude manifestations of the art, and consequently adopted a sweeping attitude towards the entire technique. But professional artists know—or at least are open to the opinion —that stenciling, like any other technique, is to be judged by its finest examples. And as we look back in the historical field we find countless specimens of stenciling that were obviously done by the best artists and craftsmen of their day. Indeed, first-rate artists have never hesitated to use stencils to achieve the exquisite and beautiful effects which they know that only stencils can give.

For our present purpose, stenciling means the application of bronze powders through a stencil made of architect's tracing linen, on to a varnished surface that is partly dry. Black is usually the background color, since this provides the beautiful deep shadows that give depth and roundness to the shaded fruits, flowers, leaves, etc.

A chair belonging to Mr. and Mrs. George E. Jones of East Hartland, Connecticut will serve excellently for the demonstration which follows.

To Trace Stencils for the Jones Chair Pattern (Figure 3, Illustration 1).

Architect's tracing linen, which we use for our stencils, is semi-transparent, thus enabling us to trace a design directly on it. The tracing is done on the dull side of the linen with a crow-quill pen and black drawing ink. Turning to Figure 3, we find the units for the chair pattern. The black areas are the parts to be cut out.

When tracing, allow at least *one inch* margin of linen around each unit. Small units may be traced two on a piece of linen, but be sure to allow an inch of linen between them. For convenience, trace the two

FIGURE 3   STENCILS FOR THE JONES CHAI

2

3

4

5

6

7

8

9

10

11

12

13

14

15

16

1

17
SAVE THIS
INSIDE PIECE
OF LINEN

18
HAND GRIP

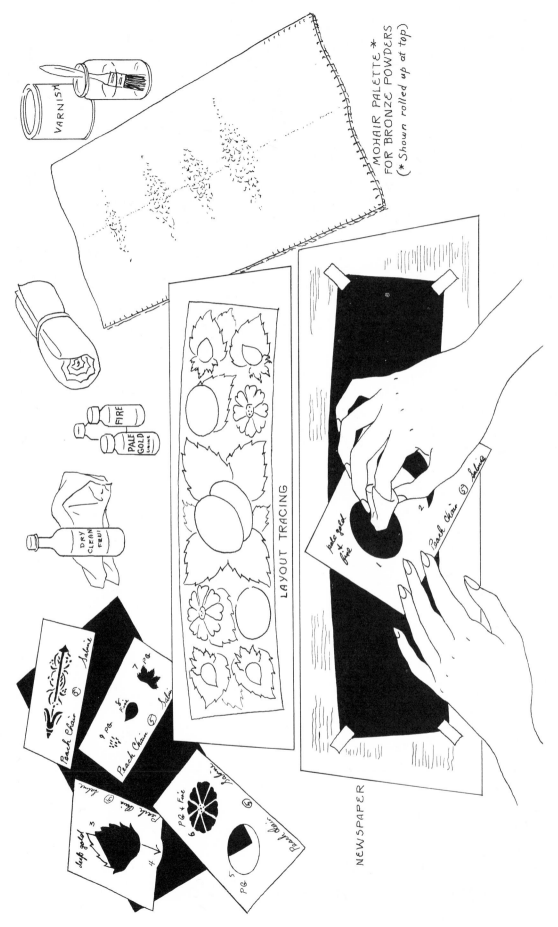

FIGURE 4 STENCILING A CHAIR PATTERN

parts of the peach on one piece of linen. Do not bear down too heavily on the pen, or you will get a thick line. The units for the stile, seat front, and narrow slat, are on Figure 37. Above all, trace carefully and accurately.

Number the stencil units in ink to correspond with the numbers in Figure 3. Refer to p. 13 for the proper care of stencils. For your own convenience, count the total number of linen pieces when you have finished tracing, and write that figure on each piece, together with the pattern's name (make up a name if you like). Also, sign your own name on each piece. See the illustration of stencils given in Figure 4. Illustration 1 shows the finished pattern and the relative positions of the units on a chair.

To Cut Stencils

Careful, accurate cutting is essential for a fine stencil job. Take the time, and exercise the patience to do it well. Provide yourself with a comfortable chair, a good light right over your shoulder, and the proper scissors (see p. 14). Be comfortable and relaxed. A black cloth on your lap will make it easier to see what you are doing, and at the same time catch the bits that fall.

In cutting, be careful not to stretch the edges of the linen cutouts. Do not pierce the cloth on the traced line, but rather inside of it. Take small snips as you go along, leaving no jagged edges. For a leaf vein, pierce the cloth in the middle, then cut towards the pointed ends. For a tiny dot, pierce the cloth with just the point of the scissors, then take five or six tiny cuts around. In a unit made up of many pieces, such as the one numbered 12, cut the smallest bit first, gradually working up in order of size to the largest one.

Making a Layout Tracing

Cut a piece of tracing paper to $13\frac{1}{2}$ by $3\frac{5}{8}$ inches for the main slat. Fold it in half to get the vertical center line, and keep it folded. Turn to Illustration 1, and with a pencil draw roughly the shape of one half of the main slat on the folded tracing paper. Slope the top line down to the side, and slant the side line in a bit. The slope of the bottom line, as can be seen in the photograph, is somewhat less than that of the top line. Still without unfolding the tracing, cut along your pencil lines. Unfolded, the tracing paper should be roughly the shape of the chair slat.

ILLUSTRATION 1   CHAIR PATTERN FROM STENCILED CHAIR
Courtesy of Mr. and Mrs. George E. Jones, East Hartland, Connecticut

Now assemble your cut stencils on a dark surface (dark table top or black paper), and roughly trace in position the various pieces, using Illustration 1 as a guide. Put the tracing paper on *top* of your cut stencils in order to trace. The middle flower is slightly to the left of center.

This is your layout tracing.

Black Paper

Just as it is important to do a painted pattern on frosted acetate before applying it as a decoration to an object, so it is important to do a stenciled pattern on black paper before putting it on a chair. This is particularly important for the beginner, who should be prepared to practice the pattern not only once but several times if necessary to get a perfect result.

Cut a piece of black stenciling paper (see p. 14) to the size and shape of your layout tracing. Tack this to a half page of a newspaper, using small bits of masking tape at the corners.

Varnishing

Spread out plenty of newspapers on your work table. Set out the varnish brush, a paint rag, the brush bath (a jar half full of turpentine), and the can of varnish, which should be opened only after everything is ready. Do not shake or stir the varnish.

After carefully dusting off the black paper, and flicking the brush to get rid of any loose hairs or dust, open the can of varnish. Dip the hairs about half their length into the varnish, and, holding down one end of the black paper with the other hand, apply the varnish. Use long sweeping strokes the full length of the paper, pressing the brush down all the way.

Work so that the light falls across the paper and you can see that every bit of surface gets covered. Work quickly, taking more varnish only as you need it, but never flooding the surface. Then, without taking more varnish, go over the surface in the crosswise direction, thus making sure that there is not too much varnish in some places, and too little in others, but instead an even distribution. Last of all, with a very light touch and using only the tips of the hairs, pick up any tiny bubbles on the surface. (If there are so many tiny bubbles that you can't possibly pick them all up, it means that you have used too much varnish. Start again on a fresh piece of paper.)

Set the varnished paper aside to dry in a dust-free place until it

[*35*]

reaches the proper tacky stage. When you come eventually to varnish a chair or other object, you proceed in the same way as for varnishing the black paper.

The Tacky Surface

How long it will take for the varnished surface to reach the proper tacky stage for stenciling will depend on the amount of varnish used, and the amount of moisture in the air. Usually it takes between forty-five minutes and one hour, but on a wet day it would take longer. Do not put the varnished surface to dry by an open window, nor over a hot radiator, nor in the sunlight, as all these, in one way or another, can spoil the surface. When the surface is dry enough to feel sticky to the touch but yet the fingertip leaves no mark on the surface, it is ready for stenciling.

Stenciling

1. Open your mohair palette and put a little mound of gold powder somewhere on the lengthwise center fold.

2. Check your cut stencils to be sure they are all at hand.

3. Wrap the velvet "finger" (see Figure 4) around your forefinger, drawing the folds tightly to the back, and holding them in place with the second finger. The tiny working surface of the velvet at the fingertip should be quite smooth and about one quarter of an inch in diameter. If the size of your finger makes a larger surface than that, stencil with the side of the fingertip. (Incidentally, you should keep two or three velvet fingers exclusively for stenciling, not using them for freehand bronze work, as this latter so saturates the velvet with bronze powder as to make it of little use for stenciling.)

4. To begin stenciling, place stencil 1 (Figure 3) in position at the left-hand side, with the shiny side of the linen downward, of course. Use Illustration 1 as your guide. Press down lightly over the cut edges, to make them stick. With the velvet finger, pick up a speck of gold powder from the outer edge of the mound—so little that it is barely visible on the fingertip—and tap it once on a clean part of the mohair. Then, with a light circular (tiny circles) motion apply the powder along the inner or pointed edge of the cut stencil. Take up more powder as you need it, a speck at a time, and generally shade off to black at the outer edge. To give the gold an added luster, go back again over the brighter parts with the velvet, and apply a little more pressure so as to burnish them.

[36]

Naturally, this pressure must not be so great as to rub off the gold or scuff the surface; and it should not be applied at all to the shaded parts. Next, lift the stencil and, having placed it in position at the right-hand side, apply the powder in the same way as before.

It is important to stencil with very little gold powder at a time, because if you use too much there is no way of picking it up again from the sticky surface. Work cautiously. If you pick up too much powder on the velvet, just tap it on a clean part of the mohair palette.

Now place stencil 2 in position slightly to the left of center. Check its position by holding the layout tracing just over it without actually laying it down (but if the tracing does happen to touch the black paper, it should not stick if you have waited for the proper degree of dryness.) Put the tracing aside, and apply the powder very brightly around the edges of the stencil, gradually shading off toward the center, but leaving the center quite black. Lift stencil 2, put stencil 3 in place and apply the powder.

Next, stencil the melon (4) very bright at the top, gradually fading off to deep black *before* you reach the center flower already stenciled. It is the swift transition from very bright gold to deep black that gives depth to the pattern, roundness to the fruit, and brilliance to the finished decoration.

Continue stenciling the pieces in their numerical order, and referring to the photograph for the shading. Always stencil the brightest part first each time, then fade off to black. Always apply the gold powder with a circular motion (tiny circles) and very lightly. Do not dab it on. Above all, remember to leave some black each time, so that a unit will look as if it is partly behind the one in front.

When the stenciling is done, immediately clean both sides of the stencils with dry cleaning fluid and a soft cotton cloth, working on newspaper. They dry in a few minutes. Let the stenciled pattern dry twenty-four hours.

Pattern for the Stenciled Fruit Rocker

Figure 5 gives the stencils for the lower pattern shown in Color Plate I. This pattern is first stenciled in pale gold. Color is added at a later stage, and consists of transparent overlays of color made by mixing varnish and artist's oil colors. The order of proceeding is as follows:

1. Trace the black units on linen, disregarding all the dotted lines, both black and white. Drawings 5 and 5A together form one single

1

2

3

4

5A

5

unit, as can be seen in the photograph, and should be traced as such on one piece of linen. Don't forget the one-inch margin of linen all around. Trace drawings 1 and 2 on one piece of linen, just as they are in position in Figure 5. If you are doing this pattern for a particular chair, alter 3 if so required to fit the lower edge of your slat, first drawing it on tracing paper.

2. There will be no need to make a layout tracing for this pattern, as the arrangement is a simple one, but a tracing of the overall area of the slat would be useful in cutting your black paper. Cut a piece of black paper 20⅜ by 4⅝ inches. Round off the ends, but leave the lower edge straight.

3. Varnish the black paper, and when it is tacky, stencil the entire pattern in pale gold. Stencil the chain border first by repeating drawing 1 from one side, along the top, to the other side, keeping it always the same distance from the edge and with equal spaces between. Then add 2 in the spaces between. Next, stencil 3 along the bottom, doing first one half; after cleaning stencil on both sides with cleaning fluid, reverse it to do the other half. Unit 4 is done next, first on the left side, and is made a bright gold where the flowers are, and not quite so bright on the outer side of the stem. Reverse the stencil and do the other side.

Now place the main fruit spray in position, centering it carefully by eye. First stencil the very bright highlights on the fruits, which are indicated by the dotted white line on Figure 5, then shading off to the darker parts. Add an extra touch of gold around the outer edges to give a reflected light. Keep looking at the color plate for the shading. The two larger leaves are very bright around the edges, darker toward the center. In this spray we do not leave any parts completely black, as there will be plenty of black spaces between the fruits and leaves when we lift the stencil. However, be sure to keep the center division in the main peach fairly dark, and to retain dark shadows around the lower and outer edges of all the fruits. Note that the main stem should be brighter in some parts, darker in others. (Note in general that all shading must be done at this stage, as the transparent colors to be added later are even washes of color and will add nothing to the brightness or darkness of the pattern.) Lift the stencil.

Set pattern aside to dry for at least twenty-four hours.

4. *The transparent color overlays* are applied next. With a damp sponge, gently go over the dry pattern to wipe off all the loose gold

powder. Remove every speck of it. Then pat it dry with a clean, lintless towel.

Set out your Yellow Lake or Indian Yellow, and Prussian Blue artist's oil colors, a newspaper palette, paint rag, turpentine brush bath, a bottle cap of varnish, a showcard brush, and a quill brush. Squeeze out about ¼ inch of yellow and about ⅛ inch of blue.

Study Color Plate I. With the No. 1 quill brush, dip out three or four brushfuls of varnish, and pull in just enough yellow to make a deep, strong, but transparent yellow. Apply this to the three yellow plums, two or three strokes to each plum, using just enough of the yellow to cover the area comfortably but not flooding it. Don't putter and dabble over this operation. Do it quickly and then leave it. Also, apply the yellow to the left side of the center peach, *immediately* blending off the inner edge of the yellow with another quill brush dipped in clear varnish. To do this, first dip the brush in varnish, and then wipe it back and forth on the newspaper to remove excess varnish, flattening the brush at the same time. With the flattened edge, go along the inner edge of the yellow, thus fading off the color, with one stroke of the brush. Do the same with the second peach. Work quickly.

Now, using the yellow quill brush, mix a transparent green by adding a little blue to the yellow. Referring to the color plate, apply this green to the leaves, each time blending off the inner edge of the color.

Set aside to dry at least twenty-four hours.

5. To apply the transparent red, use Alizarin Crimson and add a touch of Burnt Umber. Apply this to the cherries and the small flowers at the ends. Turn the whole pattern upside down and apply red to the large center peach as shown in the color plate, blending off the inner edge where it meets the yellow with a varnish brush. Do the same to the remaining peach. Set the work aside to dry for twenty-four hours.

Stenciling on Stained and Varnished Furniture

It is possible to stencil on dark furniture without first painting the background in the way described in Chapter 13. But only furniture of very dark woods should be chosen for this purpose, such as the darker forms of mahogany, walnut, oak, etc. A dark background is necessary to give the effect of the deep shadows which are a distinctive part of this type of ornamentation.

The first step is to wash the surface thoroughly with warm water and a mild soap or detergent, so as to remove every vestige of grease, wax, or furniture oil that may have been used in the past. Let the surface dry out thoroughly for a day. Then apply a coat of varnish, and when it is tacky, stencil the decoration.

To Stencil a Chair

After the chair has been painted with the background color (see Chapter 13), and before any stenciling is done, the broad gold bands should be applied. Look at Illustration 2, and observe that the turnings on the stiles (the posts on either side of the chair back) are done in gold, also some of the turnings on the legs, on the front rung, and on the hand grip. The finer stripes, not as bright as the gold, are painted mustard yellow.

The gold bands should be painted on the flat background paint with a showcard brush and a mixture of Japan Vermilion and varnish. When the surface is tacky, gold powder is applied in the usual way. After the work is thoroughly dry, remove all loose gold powder, and then proceed with the stenciling, but varnish only those parts which are to be stenciled that day. When all the stenciling has been completed, the chair is given a coat of varnish, on which, when dry, the fine mustard yellow stripes are painted with a striping brush (see Chapter 16).

The placing of the gold bands and the yellow striping depends more or less on the construction of the chair, and should be done so as to enhance the rest of the ornamentation and the general appearance of the chair.

When stenciling the main design on a chair, lay the chair on its back on your work table. Work upside down, placing the pattern you are copying upside down also.

[*41*]

ILLUSTRATION 2   STENCILED HITCHCOCK-TYPE CHAIR
Courtesy of the Society for the Preservation of New England Antiquities

8

Country Painting

The basic brush strokes for Country Painting are the same as for Freehand Bronze, and are described in Chapter 5. The student should review that chapter and practice the brush strokes on tracing paper before going on to the patterns described below. Chapter 4 ("The Painting of Patterns") should also be read over again. A good idea of the style of country painting can be obtained by looking at Color Plate V.

Tin Box Pattern (Figure 6)

This pattern was taken from a small black tin document box belonging to Mrs. John G. McTernan. The sketch shows how the various parts of the box were decorated. Proceed to paint as follows:

1. With a mixture of Japan Vermilion and varnish, paint the two large flowers and the eighteen buds, marked V, disregarding the overtone strokes shown as dotted and line-shaded areas. The mixture should contain enough varnish for it to dry smooth and flat, and at the same time give a bright opaque vermilion color. Clean the mixing brush and the quill brush by wiping them first on newspaper to remove most of the paint, and then dousing them up and down a few times in the brush bath. Afterwards wipe them dry with a cotton cloth.

2. Squeeze out some Japan Green and a tiny bit of Raw Umber. With the showcard brush, mix some Green with a little varnish, and pull in a speck of Raw Umber to tone down the Green a bit. With this "country green" mixture, and using a quill brush, paint the large and small leaves, the stems, and the calyxes on the two large flowers, all of which are shown black in the illustration. But do not paint the curlicues. This completes the present stage. Set your work aside to dry for at least twenty-four hours.

3. To paint the shaded and dotted overtones on the flowers and

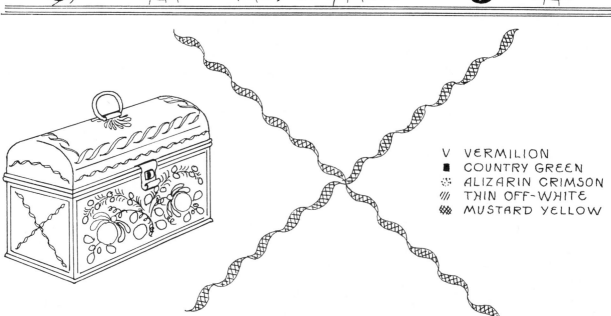

V VERMILION
■ COUNTRY GREEN
❀ ALIZARIN CRIMSON
/// THIN OFF-WHITE
❀ MUSTARD YELLOW

buds, do not put the frosted acetate over the tracing, but keep it separate. These overtone strokes are done by eye, using the illustration as a guide. On a clean newspaper palette, mix several brushfuls of varnish with a little Alizarin Crimson and just a touch of Burnt Umber, to make a rich, dark, but semi-transparent red. With this mixture, paint the dotted strokes, using your quill brush. Be sure not to overload your brush.

4. Mix some Japan Yellow with a little Burnt Umber to make a rich mustard yellow, and enough varnish to give it just a hint of semi-transparency when it is painted. With this mixture, paint the cross-hatched small leaves. Using a small quill, paint the curlicues. This will require a certain amount of practice to do correctly. Hold the brush upright, and be careful not to overload it with the paint mixture.

Add a bit more varnish to the mustard to make it semi-transparent, and paint the fine vein-like strokes on the larger green leaves, also the borders and the brush strokes that comprise the decorations on the top and sides of the box. Wait at least twenty-four hours for this to dry.

5. For the semi-transparent off-white overtones, squeeze out some Titan White and a little Raw Umber on a clean newspaper palette. Dip out several showcard brushfuls of varnish and pull in a little of the White, and a tiny bit of Raw Umber to make a semi-transparent off-white. With this mixture, and using your quill brush, paint the line-shaded strokes on the flowers and buds. The mixture should be so thin that the off-white looks slightly pinkish after it is painted on the vermilion. Be sure not to overload your brush. This completes the pattern, which should now be allowed to dry for at least twenty-four hours.

Small Chest Pattern (Figure 7)

This pattern comes from a small Connecticut Chest which is owned by Mrs. J. Woodhull Overton, and which is exhibited in the Metropolitan Museum of Art, New York. See Illustration 3 and Figure 8.

The chest is in dark oak, which may be represented by using brown paint, and the design is done in off-white, red, and black. It has been necessary to give the pattern in a reduced size on Figure 7, but as the design is a very simple one, it can be easily enlarged, as described in Chapter 18. In enlarging a pattern, enlarge only the main lines and shapes, disregarding small details such as those on the

VERMILION
BLACK
SEMI-TRANSPARENT
WHITE

FIGURE 7 SMALL CONNECTICUT CHEST PATTERN

birds. Such details can be drawn in later by eye. The original design is not exactly the same on both sides of the center line, but the differences are trifling. Therefore, you need enlarge only half the design. Thus, if you make a tracing of the left half, you have only to turn this over and you have the right half also. Join this to the left, and the whole design is before you. Measurements of the design on the front of the chest are 25½ by 13¼ inches.

For practice, it would be well to paint the enlarged pattern on a piece of frosted acetate. After you make your enlarged tracing, place it on a white cardboard so that you can see the design clearly, and then place the frosted acetate over that. Proceed to paint as follows:

1. With a mixture of Titan White, a little Raw Umber, and a little varnish, paint all the off-white parts of the design, with the exception of the stems, which are best left for another day. Disregard the monogram, the date, and the details on the birds, but paint the fine lines springing from the heads of the birds. Wait twenty-four hours.

2. Make a tracing of the outlines of the birds, and then draw in the details freehand, using Figure 7 as a guide. Be sure you get a nice swing to the wings. Then transfer these details to the pattern

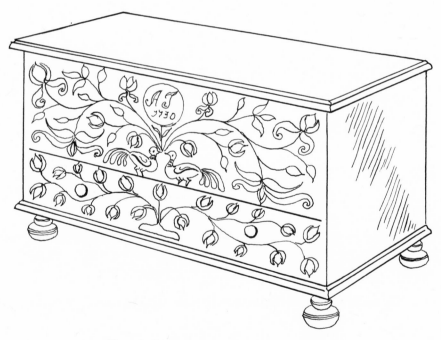

FIGURE 8　SMALL CONNECTICUT CHEST

ILLUSTRATION 3   PATTERN FROM A SMALL CONNECTICUT CHEST
Courtesy of Mrs. J. Woodhull Overton and The Metropolitan Museum of Art

(see Chapter 15). Do the same for the monogram and date, whether they are the originals or others which you may prefer to substitute. Then, using Japan Black, paint in the black details: these are the throat bands, the wing outlines, and the eyes. If you find it easier, do the eyes in pen and ink.

3. The dotted areas in Figure 7 are an almost-transparent off-white, and should be painted with one or two quick strokes of the brush. Don't fuss over this—do it and leave it. The almost transparent off-white is mixed by starting with several brushfuls of varnish, and then pulling in a little White and a speck of Raw Umber. Wait twenty-four hours.

4. Mix some Japan Vermilion with a little Burnt Umber, just enough to tone down the red slightly, and paint all the line-shaded areas in the pattern on Figure 7. For the red details on the birds' bodies, the tail marks, and the monogram and date, thin the Vermilion just a bit by adding a little more varnish to the mixture. Wait twenty-four hours.

5. Mix some off-white as near to the shade you used in stage 1 as possible, but with a bit more varnish in it to make the mixture a little thinner, and paint the stems. Use a small striping brush for this purpose, and practice a few times on tracing paper placed over the pattern. This completes the pattern.

Final Notes

When the pattern is being painted on a chest, I suggest giving the whole design a coat of varnish before painting the stems; then, if you don't get a stem just right the first time, you can rub it off for a second attempt, without disturbing the brown background color. Striping for the chest might be done in Vermilion.

9

Gold Leaf

The most essential requirement for laying gold leaf is to have such complete control of your quill brush that you are able to paint a pattern with perfect brush strokes: there should be no overly wet places, no lumpy surfaces, no touched up spots, no spreading of the color mixture after the design has been painted; but the surface should dry perfectly smooth. To acquire this proficiency, you should first copy all the gold patterns in the book on to frosted acetate, using pale gold powder. When you can do those patterns to perfection, only then are you ready for gold leaf.

Gold Leaf Booklets

Gold leaf is made up for sale in two kinds of small booklets. In one, the leaf is mounted on tissue paper; in the other, it comes unmounted. When learning to lay gold leaf without the personal guidance of a teacher, one should start with the mounted kind.

Cut a piece of cardboard the size of the booklet, and lay the booklet on it. This not only keeps the leaves flat but makes the booklet easier to handle. When not in use, keep book and cardboard in a small envelope.

Flat Background

Like freehand bronze, gold leaf decoration requires an absolutely dry background of flat or dull paint, and preferably one that has hardened for at least two months.

To Prevent Sticking

Gold leaf has a decided tendency to stick where it is not wanted, and it is for this reason that I advise two months, or even longer, for the background paint to harden.

An added measure of precaution, and a very important one, is to take a *pinch* of whiting powder and rub it lightly with the fingertips over the painted surface just *before* you transfer the pattern outlines. Blow off *all* excess powder.

Underpainting for Bread Tray Pattern

To practice laying gold leaf, put a piece of frosted acetate over sections D and E of the Bread Tray pattern in Figure 22. Illustration 6 shows this tray, which belongs to Dr. and Mrs. Roswell P. Barnes.

With a semi-transparent mixture of varnish and Yellow Ochre oil color, paint the two units, ignoring the pen-line details and the heavy black accents which indicate the Burnt Umber which later on will be applied over the gold. We use oil color because the linseed oil in it will slow up the drying process and will therefore allow more time at the tacky stage. Use just enough Yellow Ochre to give the varnish a definite color, but not so much as to make a lumpy surface.

In each unit, paint first the larger parts, then the next size, and so on down to the fine stems and tiny strokes which come last. Try to work so that the whole unit will reach the tacky stage at the same time. Set the pattern aside to dry, but keep watching it, and when the proper tacky stage has been reached, that is, when it feels sticky to the touch but you leave no fingerprint, lay the gold leaf.

Laying Gold Leaf

Pick up a mounted piece of gold leaf, holding it by the tissue paper with both hands, and with the gold side down. Hold it just above the painted design until you know exactly where you want it. Then lay it down on the tacky surface, and with your fingertips, or a clean piece of velvet, press it down, but very gently. Then lift up the tissue and, with the gold remaining on it, proceed to the next section of the pattern, slightly overlapping the leaf as you apply it, and continue in this way. With the bits that may still remain on the tissue, go back to touch up any places that may not have been covered.

Wait three or four hours, and then gently remove the loose gold with a clean piece of velvet. Let the whole thing dry for forty-eight hours. Then complete the pattern as described below.

Touching Up

When decorating a tray or any other object, you will find that after the gold leaf has been laid and allowed to dry thoroughly for forty-eight hours, there are places still without gold on them. These must be touched up. Take a quill brush, dip it in varnish, and then work it back and forth once or twice on the newspaper palette so that only a little varnish remains on the brush. With this go over the bare spots. When the spots are tacky, which in the case of very tiny spots may take only a few minutes, lay the gold leaf. The whole job should then dry for a week.

Protective Coat of Varnish

Before completing the pattern on a tray or other item, it is useful to apply a protective coat of varnish over the gold leaf. Dust off the surface, taking care to remove any remaining loose bits of gold leaf. Apply a coat of varnish in the usual way (see p. 35). Let it dry twenty-four hours, and then go over it lightly with #000 steel wool, applying just enough pressure to take off the high gloss. This will provide a good surface for pen lines and any further painting.

To Complete the Bread Tray Pattern

With a somewhat dark mixture of Burnt Umber and varnish, paint the details indicated in Figure 22 by the fine pen lines and the heavy black accents.

10

Gesso and Gold Leaf

Gesso for Raised Effects

On many of the old pieces that were decorated with gold leaf use was made of gesso to obtain raised effects. In the seventeenth century gesso was largely used for the raised decorations on the familiar gilt furniture of that period, which decorations took the forms of elaborate scrolls, birds, flowers, shells, cupids, and suchlike emblems. Pieces of the kind are often mistakenly spoken of nowadays as carved furniture, but the fact is that the raised effects were more often achieved by the use of gesso than by the carving of wood.

During the eighteenth and nineteenth centuries, gesso was widely used in the elaborately modeled ornamentation of ceilings, walls, gilded mirror and picture frames, as well as on furniture, caskets, boxes, screens, sconces, etc. The highboy in Illustration 16 shows gesso used as a means of accenting the gold decoration in the form of a low relief.

Origin of Gesso

In ancient times it was realized that to enhance the beauty of gilding on carved wood, it was necessary first to prepare a perfectly smooth surface, and it was discovered that the best way to achieve this was by the application of half-a-dozen or more coats of parchment size mixed with whiting. From this method of surface priming the use of raised gesso in ornamentation was evolved.

Composition of Gesso

As a rule, gesso is composed of three ingredients—whiting, plaster of Paris, and glue; but variations are sometimes made to produce a gesso suitable for special purposes. As a matter of interest, gelatine, boiled linseed oil, resin, marble dust, sugar, wax, starch, pipeclay, and powdered pumice have all at one time or another been used. But none of these directly concern our present purposes.

The basic method of making gesso has changed little in the course of centuries, for it would be hard to improve on the original method, and indeed some has lasted for centuries when properly made. Its earliest known use is said to have been for the priming of the wood and canvas panels used by the early painters in oils and tempera. An artist's training then included learning to make gesso. Today's artists, however, do not make their own gesso. It can be bought ready mixed in a jar.

Japanned Highboy

Though there are several ways of using gesso for decoration, we shall now discuss only the kind of decoration seen on the japanned highboy in Illustration 16. There gesso is found used to form a low relief. In this type of decoration, the pattern is traced or sketched on the painted surface, and gesso is applied with a paint brush.

Consistency

Gesso should be the consistency of very thick cream, flowing only slightly from the brush and thick enough to keep whatever shape is given to it by the brush strokes. If it shows a tendency to sink or flatten out after it is applied, the mixture is too thin. In that case, leave the gesso jar standing uncovered for a time, or add to the mixture some dry finely powdered whiting. Experiment first on odd pieces of wood or cardboard.

Brushes

The brush to use for the smaller areas is a fine scroller, which is a pointed brush with hairs about one inch long. For large areas a small-size flat oil brush is good. Very fine details like hairline strokes cannot well be painted in gesso, as the successive coats tend to broaden the fine lines.

The Relief Effect

Since the aim is to get a relief effect, don't be timid. Gesso invariably flattens as it dries, so there is little risk of overdoing the surface modeling. Several coats are usually necessary, and each coat must be thoroughly dry (several hours wait) before the next is applied.

Surface modeling should be ignored until several coats have been applied. Then a small sharp penknife, or a linoleum block cutter, or some other small blade to the use of which your hand is accustomed, may be used to scrape out here and there to add emphasis to the wing of a bird, the pack on the camel's back, the sleeve with hand resting on a table, etc. Tiny pieces of sandpaper may be used to smooth out the parts that need it. Obviously, experimental practice on scrap wood or cardboard is called for.

When the gesso work is completed and thoroughly dry, gold leaf is applied, as described in Chapter 9.

11

Stenciling on Walls

The Josiah Sage House

There can be no better introduction to stenciling on walls than to visit one of the best surviving examples of this old art. Let me describe my visit to the Josiah Sage House, which you may find it possible to visit some time in person.

One summer day I took the train from Grand Central Station, New York, to Great Barrington, Massachusetts. From there a car took me to Dodd Road in the township of Sandisfield, finally depositing me at the quiet hillside in the Berkshires on which stands the house I had come to see. The white house, with its reeded door moldings, and its semi-elliptical windows under the gable eaves is charmingly reminiscent of days gone by. A chimney stone bears the date 1803, but this is not the oldest part of the house, which belongs to the later decades of the eighteenth century. Its present appreciative owners, Mr. and Mrs. George E. Brookens, showed me every hospitality, and saw that I did not miss anything of interest.

That same afternoon the friendly co-operation of the family enabled me to set to work tracing on frosted acetate the beautiful old designs on the walls. A step ladder helped me to reach the frieze close to the ceiling; I got down on hands and knees to trace the border along the baseboard, where the more than friendly attentions of the two dogs and one cat added variations to the task. Very appropriately, I slept that night in the lovely old stenciled bedroom. Next morning I traced more units from a wall in the attic, where in 1815 the original craftsman had tried out some of the designs to show the effect to his employers. This man was an itinerant decorator whose name has been lost, but who had a fine sense of design, cut beautiful stencils, and knew how to use them to advantage.

Illustrations 4 and 5   old stenciled walls in the josiah sage house
Courtesy of Mr. and Mrs. George E. Brookens

Old Stenciling

Examples of old wall stenciling can be found chiefly in rural parts of Maine, New Hampshire, Vermont, Massachusetts, Rhode Island, Connecticut, New York, and Ohio. Most of these date from the first quarter of the nineteenth century when wall stenciling was chiefly in favor. The repainting and the papering of walls have in the course of time hidden or destroyed most original stencil work. Restoration, when possible, is always difficult. Today, however, great interest is being taken in preserving the interesting and beautiful remains of this once flourishing American craft.

Inspired by Wallpapers

The high cost of the French and English wallpapers imported during the eighteenth century, led to domestic production of wallpapers, but even these were so expensive that very few were able or willing to pay the price. It was in these circumstances that the idea of stenciling on walls arose, and it is not surprising to note that the influence of wallpaper is clearly discernible in the old stencil patterns. But since stenciled walls could imitate wallpaper only to a limited degree, they developed a style of their own, the chief characteristics of which are a certain bold conception of design, and the use of clear flat colors without shading.

The Journeyman Artist

The work was usually done by journeymen artists, working singly or in pairs, who traveled from place to place in search of patronage. One can easily imagine the importance of the occasion to a household when the artist arrived, unpacked his kit of dry colors, brushes, measuring tools, chalk, and above all his supply of stencils cut from thick paper. We can picture the eager audience standing around, watching him mix colors, helping him to choose designs and to decide the arrangements, and perhaps even giving him a hand in the actual stenciling.

Design Forms

The designs stenciled on walls by the old artists were quite varied in form, including flowers, leaves, running vines, acorns, pineapples, hearts, weeping willow trees, American eagles, urns filled with flowers, swags with bells and heavy tassels, sunbursts, diamonds, and classical motifs. Borders usually framed windows, doors, and cupboards. Wall spaces sometimes carried just a delicate border design around the edges. Broad wall spaces were often divided into panels, or given an all-over design treatment. The overmantel, being a focal point in a room, generally received some special treatment in design arrangement.

Colorings

Most of the colors used in the old stenciling have faded considerably, but the indications are that strong rich colors, such as bright reds, dark greens, deep yellow, rose, olive green, black, and occasionally dark blue were preferred. Background wall colors were usually light, and included white, grays, yellow ochre, pink, and pale blue.

For those of us who stencil walls today, it is usually advisable to avoid stenciling designs in the darker colors, and to use instead paler ones, so that there is not so much contrast in value between the stenciled motifs and the background. This color scheme would be more in tune with modern decorating trends, and it meets our need for restful surroundings in an age when mechanism and speed have made life more complex and exacting than it was in the days of the original stencilers. Some suggested color schemes are as follows:

Green and salmon pinks on white, gray, or buff walls.
Olive green and light red on pink walls.
Delicate charcoal gray borders on blue walls.
Apple green and rose on white or pale yellow walls.
Dark gray and salmon pink on pale blue walls.
Dark green and light green on pink walls.
Dark blue and medium blue on pale yellow ochre walls.

Add a little brown to all colors to "antique" them, and add white to make them paler.

To Stencil a Room of Your Own—
Preparation of Wall Surface

Go over the plaster walls, filling in any cracks or holes with patching plaster. When dry, sandpaper the surface. Then apply two coats of good quality flat paint to the walls, allowing at least twenty-four hours for each coat to dry. Save some paint for touching up later on. Also, and this is important, paint some sheets of shelf paper or pieces of masonite, on which to try out colors and to practice stenciling.

[59]

FIGURE 9   STENCILED SITTING ROOM OF THE JOSIAH SAGE HOUSE

[60]

FIGURE 10   WALL STENCILS FROM THE JOSIAH SAGE HOUSE

COUNTRY GREEN
RED
CANARY YELLOW

FIGURE 11 WALL STENCILS FROM THE JOSIAH SAGE HOUSE

VASE & FLOWERS
24¾" HIGH

■ COUNTRY GREEN
□ RED
▦ CANARY YELLOW

FIGURE 12   WALL STENCILS FROM THE JOSIAH SAGE HOUSE

Planning the Decoration

Figures 10, 11, and 12 give the stencil units traced from the sitting room and bedroom of the Josiah Sage House. Figure 9 and Illustrations 4 and 5 show them in position on the walls of the house.

In the bedroom, the running borders (Figure 10) were stenciled first: the pineapple frieze A around the ceiling, the acorn border B around the baseboard, and the red berry border C around the windows and doors as far as possible, and also at the corners of the room. The two little odd panels which are shown in the photograph with the chest of drawers below them, were given special consideration, border D running around the upper panel, C around the lower one. The single design units were then stenciled in the spaces between. The running vine C was further used to divide the larger wall spaces into panels about twelve to fifteen inches wide.

In the sitting room, a similar procedure was followed. The frieze of bells, swags, and tassels E (Figure 11) was used around the ceiling; the flower border G (Figure 12) around the baseboard and at the top of the fireplace; borders H and K around the doors and windows, and to divide the larger wall spaces into panels; border F (Figure 11) was used around two small panels similar to those in the bedroom. The single units were then stenciled in the panels, their choice as to size and position depending on the size and shape of the panels. Note the arrangements of units in the panels over the fireplace and to the right of it, and the panel at the extreme right in Figure 9.

Keep to the same general procedure in planning your own room. Choose the units you wish to use, and take plenty of time to decide where you will place them. For other examples of old wall treatments, refer to Janet Waring's *Early American Wall Stencils*, a book now out of print, but which may be found in most large public libraries. You may decide to stencil only one or two walls of your room, leaving the other walls plain, a course which would be in keeping with modern wall treatment.

Enlarging the Designs

The wall units are of necessity reproduced here in a reduced size. A glance at their original height or length, given in inches alongside each unit, will make plain the impracticability of reproducing such large designs in full size in a book. It is, however, an easy matter to enlarge the reductions (see Chapter 18), especially as the designs are simple straightforward ones, and have all been reduced here in the same proportion. One and one-half inches here was four inches in the original. You can enlarge as much or as little as you like. My advice would be to enlarge the units to their original sizes, large as that may seem at first glance. Have plenty of tracing paper on hand for the job. The enlarged tracing of a unit in a running border should be repeated several times on another piece of tracing paper, so as to make a strip about twenty inches long, which is a convenient size to handle in stenciling.

Next, lay out the enlarged tracings on a flat surface, and decide how much linen you will need, bearing in mind that for each unit there must be a separate stencil for each color used. Also allow for a two-inch margin of linen around each unit. It is advisable to make at least *two sets* of stencils, so that one can be cleaned while you are using the other. A stencil that must be repeatedly used tends to wear out (but keep the worn stencils as they can sometimes be used in places hard to get at, such as where there is a projection, and a piece of the stencil must be cut off).

Tracing on Linen

Tracing should be done in pen and ink on a heavy quality tracing cloth (see note on "Materials" at the end of this chapter). Pencil guide lines, made with a ruler or triangle, may be drawn on the linen to aid in keeping running borders straight.

Suppose you want to make stencils for the large vase of flowers in Figure 12. You will need three separate pieces of linen, one for each color. Place a piece of linen over your tracing of the enlarged design, and see that it is large enough to cover the whole unit and extend two inches all around. Trace the over-all shape of the vase, and all the white areas of the flowers and buds, referring to Figure 12. This linen will be for the red. Next, place another piece of linen over your tracing paper, large enough to cover the solid black parts shown in Figure 12, plus the two-inch margins, and trace all the black parts. This will be for the green. Take a third piece of linen, large enough to cover the dotted areas of the vase, and trace these. This will be for the yellow.

Follow this same procedure for the rest of the designs, with this exception. When a running border is to be stenciled close to the ceiling or along a door or window frame, allow only a one-half inch margin of linen on one side. This will make it possible to do the border close to the edge of the wall space.

Cutting Stencils

Stencils may be cut with the small stencil scissors. Take care not to stretch the linen when cutting. Good stencil cutting, with no jagged edges, is essential to a professional-looking job. The cut-out edges should be smooth; curved lines should be graceful and even; and points (as at the tips of leaves) should be sharp and neat.

Mixing Paints

Japan Colors mixed with a little turpentine are best for stenciling on walls, as they will dry with a flat effect. To get the proper mixed colors, artist's oil colors can be added. Using a palette knife or mixing brush, mix the colors in a thick creamy form on a piece of kitchen tinfoil, and, when they are thoroughly mixed, put each color in a small screw-top jar together with a few drops of turpentine on the surface to prevent a skin from forming. About four ounces of thick paint in each of the two chief colors will be needed for a medium-sized room.

Applying the Paint

For applying the paint through the stencil on to the wall, I use a good quality textile stencil brush as illustrated in Figure 1. The hairs should be an inch long. Get two or three brushes. The brush should be held at right angles to the wall, and used with a very light circular motion.

With a palette knife, remove a small amount of mixed color from the jar to a piece of tinfoil, adding a small amount of turpentine (use a medicine dropper) if needed. Pick up a little of the thick paint from the tinfoil with just the tip of the brush, then tap it on newspaper to get rid of excess color, and apply the color to the wall with a "dry" brush. Work with a light circular motion, moving the brush all the time from the outside edge of the cut-out toward the center, so that paint will not get under the stencil edge. If the mixture has been too much thinned with turpentine, or if too much paint is on the brush, or if the brush is used with too much pressure, color will seep under the linen. If this should happen, try to wipe it off with a touch of dry-cleaning fluid, or wait until it is thoroughly dry and touch it up with the background paint.

[66]

When the brush gets too stiff with dried out paint, dip it in turpentine, but be sure to wipe it dry again with a rag before going on.

Some decorators prefer a piece of velvet to a stencil brush. The velvet is wrapped around the forefinger, and the procedure is then the same as described above. A rubber finger-stall may be used to protect the forefinger from the paint.

Stenciling Procedure

Start with the stencils for the main color (which was generally green on old walls). When the first color has dried for twenty-four hours, apply the second.

When placing a stencil in position, use small bits of masking tape to hold it in place, leaving your left hand free to hold the cut-out part close to the wall while you apply the paint. Have plenty of clean rags at hand. When centering the single units within a panel, have a yardstick handy to make sure they are correctly placed.

If possible, have someone to help you. Each time a stencil is used, it must be cleaned on both sides with dry-cleaning fluid, and an assistant is particularly helpful here. An assistant can hold a plumb line (a string with a weight at the bottom) close to the ceiling while you chalk the upright lines to indicate where the borders are to go which will mark off the panels, thus making sure that they will be really straight. And, of course, in handing you things you need, an assistant can save you much climbing up and down the ladder.

Materials

A heavier linen is used for wall stenciling than for ordinary stenciling. Use Architect's Tracing Cloth, Phoenix No. 166, dull on top, glazed underneath, which is sold by the Keuffel and Esser Co., 60 East 42nd Street, New York (branches in Chicago, San Francisco, Seattle, and other large cities). It can be ordered in sheets of any size, or in twenty-yard rolls, thirty and thirty-six inches wide, suitable for teachers or groups.

The type of brush best fitted to this work has been described earlier in this chapter under "Applying the Paint."

Additional Designs

Since designs *in situ* are rare, and access to private homes cannot always be obtained, it may be useful to note here that the Museum of the Society for the Preservation of New England Antiquities, 141 Cambridge Street, Boston, Mass., contains the Janet Waring collection of wall stencils, and also preserves some original specimens of stenciling removed from walls and floors in old houses. Visitors may trace the photostats of the stencils, provided they bring the necessary materials with them, including frosted acetate to trace on; also, they may order prints from the negative photostats in the files. The museum is open from 9 to 4:45 every day except Saturdays, Sundays, and holidays.

12

Tinsel Pictures

Paintings on Glass

One of the most curious of the old folk art media is that of painting on glass. Pictures were painted in reverse on the back of the glass, so that the correct picture would be seen through the glass from the front. The details, therefore, were painted first, and the background last. The art flourished in this country between 1815 and 1835, the panes of glass being used chiefly to decorate shelf clocks and small or half-length mirrors. An example was taken from a wall mirror to illustrate the chapter on "Glass Painting" in my *American Folk Art* (1958). In the present book, however, a speciment is used which belongs to a slightly later period when interest had waned in the above described use of painting on glass, and had been transferred to a novel variation of the art.

Crystal or Oriental Painting

In the 1850's "Crystal" or "Oriental" painting became popular. The second name was due to the fact that the method produced effects reminiscent of the glowing colors of oriental painted flowers and birds. Flower studies were painted on glass in transparent or semi-transparent oil colors, and with opaque backgrounds. Loosely crushed tinfoil was then placed behind the painting, so that it glittered or glimmered through the glowing colors. No style of painting has ever been devised which shows off these colors to such advantage, and "tinsel pictures," as we call them today, never fail to attract admiring attention.

Pennsylvania Tinsel Picture

Color Plate VI shows a striking Pennsylvania German version. The original glass, which measures 15½ by 19½ inches, is owned by Miss Gertrude E. Robertson. The pattern given in Figures 13 and 14 is reduced in size, and would be suitable for a glass 13¾ by 10¾ inches.

There is not enough space on the figures to show all the background that appears in the color plate, but this can be added without difficulty.

To Prepare a Tinsel Glass

Procure a pane of glass as near the size of the pattern as possible. It is easier to get a framed glass to begin with, than to have a frame made to fit a piece of glass after it has been painted. Cut a piece of cardboard the same size as the glass. Take a sheet of kitchen tinfoil about two or three inches larger than the glass all around. Crush it loosely bit by bit until it is the same size as the glass. Mount it to the cardboard with bits of Scotch tape at the edges. Then cut strips of slim cardboard one-eighth of an inch wide or even less (use a ruler and a razor blade) to fit all four edges of the cardboard backing. Fasten the strips or slivers to top of the tinfoil, along the edges, by means of Scotch tape. Now place the glass on top of this (but do not fasten it), and you have a surface with glittering crushed tinfoil below on which to work. The strips of cardboard at the edges hold the glass away from the foil, and prevent the foil from being flattened out. See the inset sketch in the corner of Figure 14.

To Make a Tracing

Cut a piece of tracing paper 10¾ by 13¾ inches, and fold in half to make two halves 6⅞ by 10¾ inches. Place center fold line along the right hand edge of Figure 13, and let the top and bottom edges of the tracing paper each extend about five-eighths of an inch beyond the top and bottom of Figure 13. Make a complete pencil outline tracing of the birds and flowers, using Figures 13 and 14, but omitting the swirling background represented by dotted lines. Call this "Tracing A."

Cut another piece of tracing paper the same size, center it in the same way, and make a tracing of the background (the dotted lines) in ordinary pencil outline. Continue the background to the edge of the tracing paper. Call this "Tracing B."

To Make a Pattern on Frosted Acetate

1. Put Tracing A face down on a white cardboard. This gives you the pattern in reverse. The drawings in Figures 13 and 14 are given as they appeared from the front of the old glass picture, and have *not* been reversed. Place frosted acetate over your reversed tracing, securing it only at the top, leaving the other three sides free so that you can, in the

process of painting, place the acetate directly over the tinfoil glass to make sure your painting is transparent enough for the sparkle of the tinsel to show through.

2. The line-shaded parts of Figures 13 and 14 indicate vermilion. Compare with the Color Plate VI. The vermilion is semi-transparent in some places, opaque in others. This is achieved by working with three brushes, one with a thin semi-transparent mixture of Japan Vermilion and varnish, one with almost pure thick pigment on it, and one with clear varnish on it for blending edges. Paint a given area first with the thin mixture but don't flood it on; then *at once* dab in a few touches here and there with the thick pigment. Don't fuss over it. Do it *quickly* and then leave it. Paint one bird at a time, blending off the free edges (not the outlined ones) of the vermilion here and there with the clear varnish brush in order to soften them.

The two large flowers numbered 2 are done in the same way. (The large "mouths" of these flowers are left clear glass, as may be seen in the color plate, as are also the spaces behind the large heavy dots or pellets in all the flowers.) Continue by doing the rest of the line-shaded flowers and buds with the exception of 6. Add the opaque vermilion outline on flower 5 and on the wings, crests, and eyes of the birds; also add the large heavy dots or pellets in flowers 4, 5, 7, and in the birds' wings and tails, all of which pellets are shown in white in Figures 13 and 14.

Mix some salmon pink and paint the heavy outlines and "dabs" in each 6, and the broad band in 5; also the outline on the wings alongside the already painted vermilion one. Wait twenty-four hours for drying.

3. Look at the Color Plate VI. The semi-transparent light violet-blue areas are all outlined in a transparent dark violet-blue, made by mixing Prussian Blue with a little Alizarin Crimson and varnish. So paint the *outlines* of the flower 4 and also the six "dabs;" the outline on both sides of the pink band in 5; the outlines of the birds' necks, also around the vermilion eyes; the outlines of the four flowers numbered 9; the touches in the two small four-petaled flowers which are also numbred 9; and the outlines on the birds' wings. All the foregoing are shown as dotted areas in the drawing. The same transparent violet-blue is used for the large heavy dots or pellets in the vermilion flowers.

With Japan Black, add the black touches (shown in black in Figures 13 and 14) in the four flowers numbered 2 and 3, blending off the edges here and there in each 2.

FIGURE 13 "TINSEL" PAINTING ON GLASS

GLASS

TIN FOIL

CARD-BOARD STRIP

CARDBOARD BACKING

FIGURE 14 "TINSEL" PAINTING ON GLASS

With transparent green (Prussian Blue and Yellow Lake), paint the dark shadows on the leaves and on the birds' perches (shown in dotted white in Figures 13 and 14), blending off with a clear varnish brush here and there. These shadows are only small touches; leave most of the leaves, etc., unpainted at this stage. The downward-pointing strokes in the "mouth" of each 2 are also transparent green. Let the work dry twenty-four hours.

4. Mix Japan Green with a little Burnt Sienna to make an opaque country green, and paint all the leaves, stems, and other remaining parts shown in black in Figures 13 and 14, painting right over the transparent green already painted. This is the only color outside of the off-white in the background that has no hint of transparency. Wait twenty-four hours.

5. Mix Prussian Blue, White, and a touch of Alizarin Crimson, to make a semi-transparent violet-blue, and paint all the light violet-blue parts numbered 9 and the flower 4, leaving bits of clear acetate here and there for the tinsel to shine through (see Color Plate VI). The center of 4 behind the large heavy dots or pellets is left clear acetate.

The brown "tortoise-shell" of the birds' wings, legs, and tails is done with a transparent brown (Burnt Sienna) with darker dabs of Raw Umber here and there. The flowers 3 and 8 are done in the same way. There are also touches of "tortoise shell" in the flowers 2 and on the larger buds. The eyes on the birds are brown. Dry for twenty-four hours.

6. Remove acetate from Tracing A. Place Tracing B face down on the cardboard. Place the acetate pattern over this. Mix some White with a little Raw Umber to make an off-white, and paint the swirling lines shown by the dotted parts of Figures 13 and 14. As you can see, I have not filled in all the dots, but the fully dotted part in the lower corner of Figure 13 is enough to show you the parts to be painted off-white. What is not off-white, is left clear acetate (or glass), so that there will be plenty of tinsel highlights showing through. Use a quill-brush, held more or less vertically, and with the wrist off the ground, paint the broad lines with one stroke, raising or lowering the brush as needed. Paint also the dotted circles between the swirling lines, and the pattern is complete.

Preparing the Glass

First clean both sides of the glass with a piece of crumpled wet newspaper. Then dry them thoroughly with crumpled dry newspaper. The glass must be absolutely clean, and free from lint. Then proceed to paint the pattern on the glass according to the instruction given above for painting on the frosted acetate.

13

Preparing the Surface
for Decoration

Old Pieces of Wood or Tin

There are many pieces of old furniture and other household articles which may be nondescript, worn, and more or less treated as ready for the trash heap, but which cry aloud to the decorator for transformation. Old chests of drawers, chairs, tables of all sorts, chests, and boxes may be turned into possessions of beauty and lasting interest. And there are few jobs that give more pleasure and lasting satisfaction to the decorating artist, who knows that many people will in the course of time both use and admire what has been rescued and re-created. Now the preparation of the surface for decoration is as important as the decoration itself. So to do a good job, take time and thought. You will be glad you did.

Remove Old Paint and Varnish

Any good paint and varnish remover may be used. Read and follow the directions on the label carefully. Work with the windows open to avoid inhaling the fumes, and have plenty of old rags and newspaper at hand.

Old Wood

1. Fill in any holes or cracks with plastic wood. Let it dry thoroughly.

2. Sandpaper the flat surfaces, and rub the rounded parts with steel wool to obtain a smooth surface.

3. Apply three or four coats of flat background paint (see final section of this chapter).

[76]

New Wood

1. Sandpaper the surface, using first fairly coarse paper if the surface is very rough, then the finer paper. Use steel wool on the rounded parts and on carving.

2. Fill in crevices or holes with plastic wood. When dry, sand again.

3. Apply a coat of fresh shellac to seal the new wood. Let it dry twenty-four hours.

4. Sandpaper again with very fine sandpaper.

5. Apply three or four coats of flat background paint (see final section of this chapter).

Removing Rust on Tinware

All tinware should be treated for rust whether the latter is visible or not; for in its initial stage rust is invisible. For this purpose we may use Rusticide. Clean the surface first, removing any dirt and grease. Apply Rusticide with a one-inch bristle paint brush. Wait five minutes, and then go over the surface with steel wool. If the metal is badly rusted, use a second application and leave it on a little longer, making sure that sufficient Rusticide is on the surface to keep the rust wet and thus ensure penetration. Heavy accumulations of rust may require several applications and scrubbings with steel wool to remove the dissolved rust. Wipe off with a clean cloth. The metal should then be perfectly clean and sealed against fresh oxidation, thus providing an excellent base for the primer paint. Allow to dry overnight, and begin painting the next day. If it is necessary to paint immediately, wipe off the surface with alcohol. Although the surface will not immediately re-rust, it is advisable to apply paint with as little delay as possible.

Primer Painting on Tinware

Never paint a piece of tinware without giving it one or two coats of a good primer paint (see Chapter 3), or the paint will not stick properly. Be sure the primer paint has been thoroughly mixed. The first coat of primer paint may be used straight from the can if it is fairly thin, but if it seems overly thick, thin it a little with turpentine. Apply it as you would a background coat of paint (see below). The second coat may be thinned a bit more. On large flat surfaces it should be applied in a crosswise direction to the first coat. When the primer coats are completely dry, sandpaper the surface until it is perfectly smooth to the touch. Dust thoroughly. Now you are ready for the background coats of paint.

Flat Background Painting

The mark of a professional job of background painting, whether in black or any other color, is that the surface be flat or dull to the eye, and perfectly smooth to the touch. If you feel any ridges, your paint was not sufficiently thinned with turpentine to make it a very thin and watery mixture. To sandpaper it smooth takes time and labor, and may take off too much paint in spots. Besides, it is unprofessional—that is, below the high standard we aim at. Apply the paint properly in the first place. Study the directions given below very carefully, and follow them exactly.

Before applying any paint at all, examine the object to be painted and decide how you will hold it during the process, which part you will paint first, which second, and so on. Make sure you leave one part unpainted on which to rest the object while drying. Have a place prepared on which to set the object for drying. You can see how necessary it is to attend to these matters before you apply the paint. Also, the object should be dusted off carefully before painting begins.

Open the can of black paint and stir it thoroughly with a small stick until it is completely mixed. There is usually not enough room in a fresh can of paint to add sufficient turpentine for thinning. So take a small jar, and pour into it about an eighth of an inch of turpentine, or more if you are doing a big job (be sure to give the can of turpentine a shake or two before using it, to mix it up). With your one-inch bristle brush, dip out several brushfuls of paint, adding them to the turpentine in the jar. Mix with the brush. The mixture should be quite thin and watery.

Begin to apply the paint in long even strokes, all in the same direction. Don't flood it on—use just enough to cover. Because of the thinness of the paint, the first coat will not entirely cover the surface, but don't go back to retouch any part of it. Paint it and leave it, and work quickly. Last of all, check around the edges for any dripping. Let the work dry for twenty-four hours.

In applying the second coat, paint the large areas in the opposite direction to the first coat; that is, apply the second coat crosswise to the first one, thus achieving an even result. Never apply a succeeding coat until the preceding one has dried at least twenty-four hours, and feels completely dry. Every object should have at least three coats and preferably four.

Now if you have done a proper job of sanding and preparing the wood in the beginning, and have applied the paint correctly, you should have a smooth, dull surface that needs no sanding. If it is necessary, however, sandpaper the last coat very lightly, when it is thoroughly dry, with a square inch or so of very fine sandpaper. A tiny piece can be controlled better than a large one. Avoid sanding the edges or other "vulnerable" parts, that is, parts where the sandpaper might take off the paint altogether.

Allow the final coat of paint to harden a month or longer before applying a decoration, although a shorter time is all right if you intend to do a stenciled decoration. The longer waiting period is necessary for light or colored backgrounds, or when gold leaf or bronze powders are to be used. The waiting period can be employed in brush-stroke practice, painting patterns, or in preparing other objects for decoration.

14

Background Colors

Black backgrounds are the easiest to work on, since corrections are least noticeable on black. For this reason, beginners are strongly advised to work for some time only on black, and to go on to the colored grounds later.

The paints we use for background coats are good quality flat indoor paints. By flat, I mean paints that give a dull surface. Never use glossy enamels. How to apply a coat of flat background paint has already been described in Chapter 13.

Testing a Paint

The paint manufacturers' chemists have been making changes in the composition of many paints of late, and this makes it difficult to advise which brands of paint are reliable for our purposes. A flat black that I formerly recommended to my students and readers has been changed so completely within the last few years as to become useless to us.. Recommendations of brands in this book should be understood, therefore, to be only currently valid.

It is a good idea to paint a piece of cardboard with two or three coats of a paint (if you are in doubt about it), and make a brush stroke test with the same mixtures you intend to use in painting the decoration. Also cover a section of the background paint with clear varnish. If the colors and the clear varnish sink right into the background paint so that they dry in a spotty fashion, you had better change your brand. The brush strokes should look and behave the same on the paint as they do on the frosted acetate.

Buying Paint

Another difficulty which confronts us today is in getting colors like dark brown, dark green, and red in flat paints that can be thinned with turpentine. Manufacturers are tending to stylize their colors according to the prevailing popular taste, which at present is supposed to be for pastel colors. Do not use paints that can be thinned with water. We use the kind that can be thinned with turpentine.

When you buy paint, you must know just what you want, and you must check (by reading the labels) to be sure you get what you ask for.

Mixing

Since many of our background colors have to be obtained by mixing, it is useful to save small screw-top jars for the purpose. Mix sufficient color to ensure that you will still have some left over in the jar which can be used for touching up after the decoration is on. Mix the pigments first, then add the turpentine to get the proper watery consistency (see p. 78). Mix relatively small quantities of the thick color, because the addition of the turpentine will greatly increase the quantity. Always remember when mixing colors to allow for the darkening and yellowing effect of the finishing coats of varnish.

Flat Black

For flat black backgrounds these are brands I have recently tested with satisfactory results:

Sapolin Dull Black Enamel #31, Flat Finish.

Devoe Mirrolac Flat Black.

A D Flat Black.

There are, of course, many other reputable makes, such as Lowe's and Sherwin Williams's.

Antique Black

This is characteristic of many old pieces, and might be described as an off-black or charcoal color. It is very effective in giving a job the antique look.

To mix antique black, put some Flat Black in a clean jar and add some Raw Umber and White in the following manner: squeeze a little of the Raw Umber and White on to an old saucer; dissolve them by mixing in some of the black with a showcard brush or palette knife; when no lumps remain, add the mixture to the jar of flat black and stir thoroughly with a small stick. Test the color on a piece of paper, using the showcard brush.

[*81*]

Brown

If you have difficulty in finding a good flat brown paint in your local shop, you might write to E. P. Lynch, Inc. (address on p. 16) for their Van Bellum Brown.

Any brown can be modified by adding:

Yellow to make it lighter and warmer;

Vermilion or red to make it still warmer;

Prussian Blue to make it darker and colder;

White to make it lighter.

Medium Colors

Use the nearest available color in flat paint, and add the necessary tube colors as indicated below:

1. *Antique Red.* To flat spectrum red paint (if you can get it) add Raw Umber, Japan Yellow, and a little White. Avoid using Vermilion because, in large quantities, it does not mix well with other pigments, thus making it almost impossible to get an even background color.

E. P. Lynch, Inc. have an excellent antique red already mixed, called Harreth Red.

2. *Antique Blue.* A sample of a good antique blue can be prepared on your newspaper palette by mixing White and Raw Umber together, and then adding Prussian Blue. Paint one or more samples of antique blue on a card, and take it to your paint store as a sample of what you want.

3. *Olive Green.* Olive green is made by starting with Japan Green and adding Burnt Umber and Yellow Ochre. Another olive green can be had by adding Burnt Sienna to the Japan Green.

Light Colors

Use flat white paint as a base for all light colors, adding Japan or oil colors to get the color you want.

1. *Off-White.* White with a little Raw Umber added.

2. *Gray.* White with more Raw Umber added until you get the color you want.

3. *Cream.* White with a little Yellow Ochre added.

4. *Pale Antique Yellow.* White, Japan Yellow, and Raw Umber.

5. *Pale Apple Green.* White, Japan Yellow, Raw Umber, and a touch of Prussian Blue.

[*82*]

Japan Colors

Japan colors can be used for background paints where small quantities are called for. Mix them with turpentine, adding other tube colors when necessary to get the colors you want.

Grained Backgrounds

Painted furniture was sometimes given a grained background in order to imitate expensive woods. Occasionally, graining was used on boxes. The graining was generally done in black over a dull red painted background (to imitate rosewood), or over a walnut stained background.

For "rosewood" graining, first apply two or three thin coats of dull red in the usual way. The red is a Venetian red or brownish red, made by adding a little Vermilion to flat brown paint. When the color is dry, apply a coat of rather thin flat black, and *immediately* grain lengthwise along the wood by pulling a crumpled piece of stiff muslin across the wet surface. Experiment on painted cardboard first.

Graining can also be done by using a crumpled piece of soft plastic film, or of newspaper; crushed cellophane; a piece of cardboard, or thin wood with the edge cut in irregular notches; or anything else you may have at hand that will produce the desired effect. The graining should be subdued in character or it will distract attention from the decoration.

On large pieces of furniture, apply the black in sections in order that the graining can be done comfortably before the black sets or begins to dry. On a stenciled chair, the main slat is not grained, but is painted black.

Asphaltum

A background that is often found on old tinware is asphaltum, a mixture of asphalt and varnish. It is a somewhat transparent background painted directly over the bright tin, in shades ranging from black through dark brown, and its special charm is in the hint of bright tin showing through the color. But asphaltum is difficult to apply, for it tends to show streakiness, and thus it is advisable to begin with plenty of practice on bright tin cans.

Asphaltum comes in cans, and if applied straight from the can without thinning it is completely black. So for our purposes it needs thinning, but thin it only with *varnish*. When varnish is added, the color becomes a lovely lustrous brown, darker or lighter depending on the amount of varnish added. Some decorators like to add a little Alizarin Crimson to get a reddish brown. Mix the amount you require in a separate jar.

Apply the mixture with a varnish brush (some decorators prefer a flat camel's hair brush), working quickly, and flowing it on, rather than painting it on. Use as few strokes as possible, and don't go back to re-touch. If you have enough of the mixture on your brush as you apply it, the streakiness may disapper when the asphaltum settles. If mistakes are made in applying it, the surface can be cleaned off immediately with turpentine, and another attempt made.

Asphaltum should dry for one week, after which time it can be given a protective coat of varnish, but this coat of varnish must also be flowed on, with as few strokes as possible, or you may disturb the surface.

If your tinware is no longer bright, you can simulate a bright shiny surface by applying a coat of varnish. When this is tacky, that is, not quite dry, apply aluminum or chrome powder with a piece of velvet, and then burnish the surface with a little extra pressure on the velvet. Wait twenty-four hours, wash off all the loose powder under running cold water, and pat the surface dry with a lintless towel. Then apply a coat of varnish to protect the surface. Let this dry twenty-four hours. Finally, apply the asphaltum mixture.

15

Transferring the Design

After the surface of an object has been prepared for a freehand painted decoration, there is one more step to be taken before the design is actually painted. An outline of the pattern has to be transferred to the surface as a guide. Commercial carbon papers, being greasy, are unsuited to our purpose, and so we must make our own type of "carbon" paper, as described below. Once made, these carbons can be used again and again. Preserve them for future use in a folder.

White "Carbons"

A white "carbon" is needed to transfer a pattern to a dark ground. Rub a cake of magnesium carbonate (see p. 16) over the surface of one side of a piece of tracing paper, 6 by 12 inches. Then rub the deposited powder well into the paper with the fingertips. Blow off the excess powder. Fold the tracing paper in half, with the powdered surface inside, and put this in a book, so that there is some pressure on it. Leave it there for a week, during which time the powder will work into the paper. A second white carbon, about 4 by 8 inches, is useful for the smaller jobs.

Dark "Carbons"

For transferring a design to light backgrounds you will need a dark "carbon," which can be made by penciling all over one side of tracing paper with the flat side of the lead of an H or 2H pencil. Do not use a soft, smudgy pencil. There is no need to rub the penciling in, and the carbon can be used immediately without any waiting period.

Trace the Design

Make a careful tracing on tracing paper of the design you intend to use. Include everything but the superimposed details which can be added later by eye. Use a well-sharpened H or 2H pencil.

Transferring to a Dark Background

Place your pencil tracing of the design in position on the surface to be decorated. Make sure the design is exactly where you want it to be, for carelessness at this stage will spoil the whole job. Stand up to place the design, so that you can see everything to better advantage. Don't rely on measuring with a ruler, for most patterns are not exactly alike on both sides. Consider not only the tracing, but also your finished copy on frosted acetate, so that you can judge the "weighting" of the pattern. Be sure the tracing is not tipped to one side or the other.

When it is just right, secure the tracing to the surface with two or three tiny pieces of masking tape, placed so that you can slide the carbon, white side down, underneath the tracing without distrubing the tape.

Now retrace the design over the carbon with a well-sharpened 3H pencil, exerting some pressure in the process. Pick up one corner of the carbon from time to time to make sure you are getting a white outline on the painted surface. Move the carbon along, when and if necessary, to keep it under the pencil point. When the transfer is completed, you are ready to paint the pattern just as you did in your frosted acetate copy.

Transferring to a Light Background

Proceed as for a dark background, using your pencil carbon instead of the white one.

Stencil Patterns

The above instructions are all for free-hand painted designs, or parts of designs, such as the free-hand gold parts of the stenciled cornice in Color Plate III. The carbons are of no use in stenciling a design. See Chapter 7, "Stenciling."

16

Striping

Striping is not the difficult thing it appears to be at first glance. A little practice and determination are all that are required, and they will be amply rewarded. Nothing gives such a professional finish to your work as a nice bit of striping.

Although not every old piece was striped, the majority of them were. For this reason, and because of the added embellishment, it is recommended that you stripe everything you decorate.

Function

The function of striping is further to enhance the appearance of the decoration, and to put a finishing touch to the whole piece. Although striping is always in a contrasting color to the background, it should never be so prominent that it distracts the eye away from the main decoration, or from the piece as a whole. In a word, striping should not be conspicuous.

With this in mind, we keep the gold or bronze powder stripes from getting too wide. Usually they should not be more than one-eighth to three-sixteenths of an inch wide on the very largest objects that you decorate. For very fine or hairline stripes, which should not be wider than one-sixteenth of an inch at the most, we generally use a Japan color. And in the case of red, green, or yellow, we add one of the browns (oil colors) to subdue the color, adding quite a lot of brown in the case of yellow.

Striping Colors

1. *On Black Backgrounds.* When the background is black, and the main decoration is in a gold technique, the striping is usually in gold too. These gold stripes are usually accompanied by a fine mustard yellow stripe made on the inner side. A gold stripe is made by striping first

[*87*]

in Yellow Ochre (for gold leaf) or Japan Vermilion (for gold powder), and when the tacky stage has been reached, applying the gold.

For black grounds that have a country-painting style of decoration, striping should be in a vermilion, a mustard yellow, or a dull off-white.

2. *Off-White or Gray Backgrounds.* We seldom use a stark white background but rather add a little Raw Umber to soften the white. If you keep adding Raw Umber you will get a whole series of beautiful pale grays.

Striping should be in vermilion, dark country green, black, or brown (Raw Umber or Burnt Umber), depending on the colors in the decoration.

3. *Brown Backgrounds.* These usually have a pattern in the country style of painting, and striping should be in off-white, vermilion, or mustard yellow.

4. *Pale Yellow Backgrounds.* Striping should be in black, brown, country green, or vermilion.

5. *Red Backgrounds.* With gold decorations, the striping should in gold. With country style decorations, striping should be in black, or mustard yellow, or off white.

6. *General.* Striping colors generally reflect the prevailing color in the decoration. On some of the old chairs and trays, we find opaque stripes, while on others they are semi-transparent. In the former case, less varnish is used in the striping mixture; in the latter, more varnish.

Surfaces for Striping

Gold or other bronze powder striping should be done on the flat or dull background paint. In the case of a stenciled decoration, the gold striping should be done before the surface is varnished in preparation for the stenciling.

Colored striping, generally done with Japan color, or in Japan colors mixed with oil colors, is best laid on a dry varnished or glossy surface which will keep the stripe from feathering, and also facilitate erasures. Corrections must be made at once, with a little turpentine or dry-cleaning fluid on a rag.

Brushes

A minimum of two brushes is necessary, one for very fine striping, and one for the wider striping (see Figure 2). Stripers are square-tipped

I TWO STENCILED ROCKER PATTERNS
*Courtesy of Mr. & Mrs. Roderick D. MacAlpine, Mr. & Mrs. Carstairs
Bracey, and Mr. & Mrs. Arthur Tompkins*

II TWO CHAIR PATTERNS
*Courtesy of Mr. & Mrs. Vernon H. Brown and the New York Historical
Society*

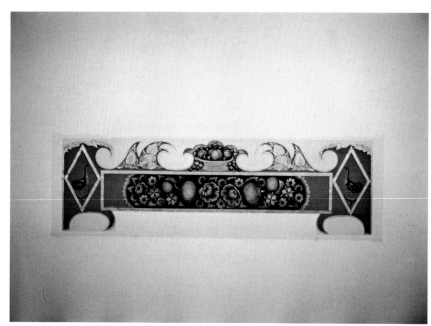

III   CORNICE PATTERN
Courtesy of the Cooper Union Museum for the Arts of Decoration

IV   ENGLISH SEWING TABLE WITH FLORAL DECORATIONS AND GOLD LEAF
Courtesy of Mr. & Mrs. Vernon H. Brown

quill brushes, with hairs one and one-half to two inches long, and are used without a handle.

Making the Stripe

In the act of striping, the brush is always pulled toward you (see Figure 15). To mix some mustard yellow for striping practice, fill a bottle cap one-third full of varnish. Using a showcard brush, add a little Japan Yellow and a little Raw Umber to the varnish until the color is a rather dark mustard yellow, and the mixture somewhat thin. Lift out a few brushfuls of the mixture on the newspaper palette. Dip the striping brush into it, moderately loading it to the full length of the hairs, and pulling it back and forth on the newspaper to get the feel of the brush.

Practice striping on a piece of the black glazed stenciling paper. The stripe should be about one eighth of an inch wide, and you should be able to stripe about a foot or two before you need to replenish the brush. To get a narrower stripe, flatten the brush on the newspaper palette, and then stripe with the thin edge of the brush.

It is also helpful to practice striping on a raw tray to get the feel of working on a hard object. The paint can easily be cleaned off with turpentine.

When striping a rectangular shape, such as the top of a box, or a chair slat, do not try to make two stripes meet in a perfect angle at the corner. Instead, carry the stripes across one another and on to the ends of the area. This done, immediately clean off the bit of unwanted striping at the intersection by wiping with a clean cloth. Or wait twenty-four hours for the striping to dry, and cover up the unwanted part with the background paint.

Furniture, or anything else you decorate, is generally striped according to the construction of the piece. For examples of this, see Illustrations 2 and 17.

17

The Finishing Coats
of Varnish

Once the decoration has been completed, including the striping, you are ready to apply the finishing coats of varnish. But first carefully inspect your work, and if any touching up is necessary—and some usually is—this is the time to do it.

Touching Up

For this purpose use the extra background paint that you saved specially. Don't stir the paint, but with a palette knife or small stick, lift out some of the thick paint at the bottom of the can and place it on the newspaper palette. If you need to thin it as you work, use the "juice" from the top of the can. Use a small quill brush or a pointed water color brush, and touch up wherever there are obvious faults which can be corrected in this way: perhaps smudges of gold powder on the background, or pointed leaves that aren't as pointed as they should be, or a stripe that needs a little straightening out. Don't do so much touching up that it becomes noticeable. Don't bother to touch up little faults that no one is likely to observe. You must use your judgment. Stand away from your work now and then to get the general effect. When touching up is finished, let the work dry for twenty-four hours.

Varnishing

To simulate the satin smooth finish found on most old pieces, we apply at least six coats of the regular high gloss varnish. On table tops or trays for which a heat or alcohol resistant surface is needed, an extra two coats is advisable. Warning: If your decoration includes the use of any bronze powders, the successive coats of varnish must be applied as soon as possible once the first coat is on, otherwise the powders will probably tarnish (see p. 29).

Antiquing

To simulate the antique coloring found on many old surfaces, we may tone one or two coats of the varnish with oil pigments. But the varnish must remain completely transparent, and so only the barest touch of color should be used; otherwise you will get ugly streaks across the surface. Oil pigments generally used for this purpose are Raw Umber or Burnt Umber, but occasionally, to get special effects, Yellow Lake, Black, or Prussian Blue are necessary. Antiquing is generally done on the first coat, or the first two coats, depending on the effect you want. Be careful not to "over-antique," as a little of this varnish goes a long way. Besides, the clear varnish naturally turns darker in a few years at most, and this is all the more reason to be very cautious indeed if you antique.

Getting Ready to Varnish

Since one great enemy of a good varnish job is dust, clean the room first, and allow the dust to settle. Close all windows and doors, and keep all traffic away for the first three or four hours after varnish is applied.

The room should be 70 degrees or warmer, and the can of varnish and the object to be varnished should have been standing in that temperature for some time. Varnish applied to a cold surface in a cold room will "crawl," that is, tend to separate or "ridge." A freshly varnished surface should be kept away from hot radiators, cold places, drafts, open windows, and direct rays of the sun.

Applying the Coats

Taking a tray as an example, proceed as follows:

First Day. Spread out plenty of clean newspapers to work on. Decide where the tray will rest in order to dry, and place newspapers there, with a tin can or other suitable object on which to set the tray. Dust off the tray, and just before varnishing wipe off with your hand, to remove any remaining dust or lint, especially in the corners.

Assuming that you want to "antique," squeeze out a little Raw Umber alongside the opened varnish can (which you ought to have standing on the clean newspaper palette). With your one-inch varnish brush, dip

[*91*]

out several brushfuls of varnish, and pulling in a speck of Raw Umber mix a puddle of "antique" varnish. Try it out on a clean piece of paper to see the color, which should be very little darker than the clear varnish itself. Work very quickly as the varnish thickens on contact with air.

Then apply the "antique" varnish to the tray in this order: first do the underside of the flange; then turn the tray over and do the edge and the top side of the flange; and finally do the floor. Work with the light falling across your work; in this way you can see that every bit of surface is covered. Don't flood the varnish on, as it will only run down and settle in the corners where it can't dry properly. Spread the varnish out with the brush, using long strokes the full length of the floor. Then, without taking any more varnish unless absolutely necessary, use the brush in the crosswise direction to ensure an even distribution. Work quickly, mixing more varnish and Raw Umber if you need to.

When you have finished, inspect the work carefully, and with a very light touch, and using only the tip of the brush, pick up any tiny bubbles and/or brush hairs which may appear on the surface. Last of all, check the underside of the tray for any varnish drippings. Let the work dry for twenty-four hours.

Second Day. After dusting off the surface, apply the second coat of varnish, adding a touch of Raw Umber only if you want a darker color. Dry for twenty-four hours.

Third Day. Dust off the surface and apply the third coat of varnish. Dry for twenty-four hours.

Fourth Day. Although sandpapering must be thorough, be careful not to do too much of it, or to apply too much pressure, as otherwise you might go right through the coats of varnish. Sand first the floor of the tray, then the flange, but keep away from the edges where you might very easily take off both varnish and paint. This caution should be observed, of course, with any kind or size of object.

Take some very fine sandpaper, and cut it into pieces about 1½ by 3½ inches, fold them in half with the sand outside, and begin to sand the floor of the tray. Sandpaper diagonally, first from upper left to lower right, then from upper right to lower left, taking only small sections at a time. When one hand is tired, use the other, thus saving time and avoiding fatigue.

When the sanding is finished, dust off the tray.

If any sand particles remain stuck in the corners, it means you used too much varnish previously, with the result that it did not dry properly. If this happens, wait another 24 hours for the corners to dry out; then sand again.

Apply the fourth coat of varnish. Let it dry twenty-four hours.

Fifth Day. Sandpaper the surface as described above with still finer sandpaper or with #000 steel wool. Dust off. Apply the fifth coat of varnish.

Sixth Day. Sandpaper the surface again. Dust off. Apply the sixth coat.

Extra Coats

Six coats of varnish are the minimum. For a really beautiful and extra smooth, satiny finish more coats are necessary. Eight or ten coats give a superb finish, although it must be remembered that extra coats tend to darken and yellow the decoration. For this reason, when extra coats are to be applied, I would not use any Raw Umber in the initial coats, or I would use a less amount than usual.

The Final Rubbing

This calls for powdered pumice, crude oil, and a cotton flannel cloth. Put about a teaspoon of the powder in a saucer. Take a small flannel cloth, put some crude oil on it, and then dip it into the pumice. Begin to rub small sections of the tray floor, a few square inches at a time, using a small circular motion. There is no need to rub long, for the high gloss of the varnish comes off immediately, and that is all you want. If you rub too long, the surface will be dull and lifeless, whereas the proper result is a satiny gleam. Use enough crude oil to keep the rubbing moist.

When you have gone over the whole surface, rub off the remains of the oil and pumice with a clean flannel cloth, and let the surface dry. If any bright glossy spots show up, give them a rubbing as before. This satin finish needs no furniture polish to preserve it, but only a damp cloth now and then. (We do not use a satin-finish varnish).

18

Enlarging and Reducing Patterns

Enlarging

Take Border 5 in Figure 2 for an example, and proceed to enlarge it as follows:

1. Trace one or two units of the border on the upper left-hand corner of a piece of tracing paper. Refer to the drawings in Figure 16.

2. Using a small right-angle triangle, or a postcard, draw a rectangle around the units which will box them in and touch them on all four sides. Use the triangle to get right-angles at all four corners, and draw the lines with a well-sharpened 2H pencil.

3. Continue the right-hand side of the rectangle downwards a few inches, and extend the bottom line out to the right several inches.

4. With a ruler or triangle, draw a diagonal line from the upper left-hand corner to the lower right one, and continue it out beyond the box, as in the illustration.

5. Measure either the width or the height of the larger size that you want (in this case it would be the height of the border), and complete the larger of the two rectangles joined by their corners as in the illustration. Use the triangle to get right-angles, and be sure that the diagonal line mentioned in the preceding paragraph passes through the lower right-hand corner. This ensures that the enlargement will be in the same proportion as the original.

6. Divide the long sides of the first rectangle in half, then in quarters, and finally in eighths. Divide the short sides into quarters. Do the same with the larger rectangle. In the case of larger and more complicated patterns, the sides could be divided into sixteenths, thirty-seconds, and so on.

[*94*]

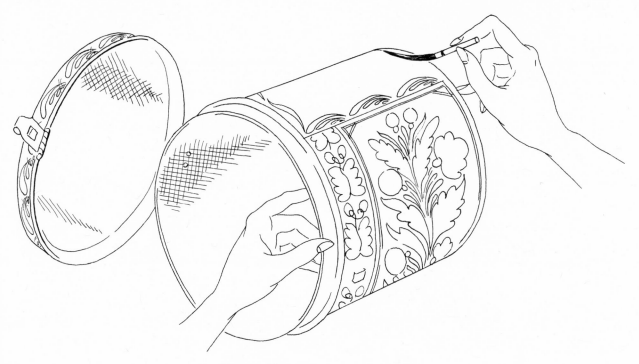

FIGURE 15   STRIPING THE CANISTER

FIGURE 16   TO ENLARGE A DESIGN

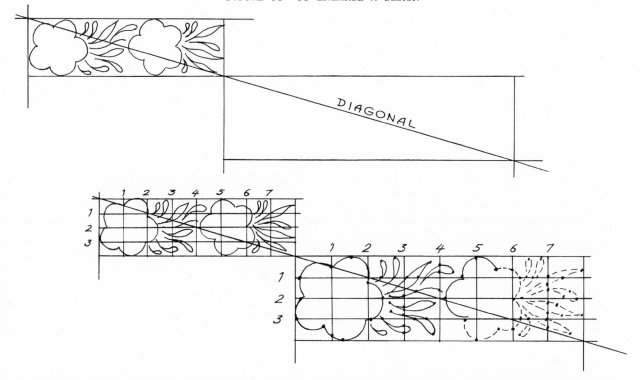

DIAGONAL

7. Rule and number the lines, as shown in the lower drawing in Figure 16.

8. The outlines of the pattern in the smaller rectangle are crossed by the ruled lines. Note where each point of intersection occurs, and put a dot at the corresponding place in the larger rectangle. When the dots are all in place, join them up with lines of the same character as those in the original.

9. If the finished drawing seems a bit stiff, place a fresh piece of tracing paper over it, and retrace it, improving the drawing as you go along.

Reducing

The general procedure is the same, but when extending the right-hand side and the bottom of the first triangle, you will, of course, make a *smaller* rectangle, corresponding to the size of the reduction you seek. By turning Figure 16 upside down, you can see how the two rectangles should look for reducing purposes.

19

How to Use the Patterns

"Good Taste"

Everyone will agree that good taste should be a guiding principle in work of this kind, and even those who are naturally gifted in this direction can cultivate their gift to a higher degree. A few ways to acquire or develop good taste in our field of decoration are:

1. Visit museums to study old pieces of ornamented furniture and smaller objects of all kinds. When you plan a vacation, try to include visits to museums at a distance from home. Your public library has reference books which indicate what museums are in particular localities, and what kind of exhibits they contain. Write to local chambers of commerce for further information. With a little preparation, vacations can be made educational as well as recreational, and if you can interest your family and friends in your plans, so much the better. Similarly, one may study old pieces in the windows of antique shops, or in private homes.

2. In studying old pieces, note the kind of ornamentation that was used, how much blank space was left around the designs, and how the designs reflect the general lines and shape of the whole piece; for example, a light, delicate, graceful design on a light, gracefully shaped chair, or a heavy, strong, bold design on a bulky chest of drawers. Note what colors were used, and how they combined to give a pleasing effect.

Have a small notebook and make entries in it. Include rough sketches. Buy photographs of the objects when these are available. All this will help you to remember what you have seen, and will form source material of special value to you.

3. Most libraries have books on antique decoration, design, and decorative arts of all kinds. Some may be taken home for perusal, others must be read in the reference rooms of the libraries. Making yourself familiar with such books will help enormously in cultivating a sense of

what looks well and what doesn't. If your budget allows you to buy some art books, that is all to the good, for books which are at your elbow and you consult constantly become, in a sense, part of you.

4. If you are decorating objects which are reproductions of old pieces, or old pieces whose decorations have worn off, it is particularly important to use appropriate designs. A tin box should have a tin box design, a chair a chair design, and a tray a tray design. Size and type of design will be carefully considered in relation to the size and type of article. In ornamenting modern pieces with the old patterns, greater freedom may be used in the choice and placing of designs, but of course good taste remains an indispensable ingredient of the work.

To Enlarge or Reduce a Design

Naturally, there are times when a design must be enlarged or reduced to fit a certain space. Here the required caution is to avoid extremes. Choose a design as near as possible to the size you need. For the method of enlarging and reducing see Chapter 18.

To Adapt a Design

If you need to adapt a design for use on an area the size and shape of which are somewhat different from that of the original, proceed as follows:

Mark off on a sheet of tracing paper the area you want to decorate. Put this tracing over the original pattern, and proceed to make a revised drawing of the pattern according to your needs, moving the tracing paper about so that different parts will appear where you want them. Draw in the larger or more important parts first, then the secondary parts, and finally the least important parts or the "fill-ins." As you work, add to or leave out parts of the design as needed. These changes should be made by eye, care being taken to preserve balance and good proportion in the whole design. As a general rule, however, change the original design as little as possible.

20

The Happy Artist

When our efforts in any direction are crowned with success, we are able to look back upon the whole process with a feeling of happiness. But since success in any field depends on following the proper "recipe," on knowing the "tricks," or the "secrets of success," I set down below a few hints and suggestions that my pupils and I have found helpful. Some of these will seem prosaic, not to say commonplace. But these commonplace principles, when applied faithfully, are the key to that sustained endeavor which leads us to successful results.

1. Learn to criticize your own work by looking back on what you did the day before, and picking out the flaws, the downright mistakes, all the things that might have been better. Praise from those around you is very sweet, but don't let it keep you from sternly criticizing your own work.

2. Strive for ultimate perfection in everything you do. Endeavor to trace an outline exactly. Try to paint a pattern exactly as it should be done. Follow instructions precisely.

3. At the same time, deliberately cultivate a mental attitude of patience. The learning process takes a certain amount of time. Be willing to do a thing as many times as it may be necessary in order to get it right. And just as deliberately maintain a happy frame of mind while learning and doing.

4. Practice is essential in learning a new skill. But just as important is your mental attitude while you practice. Always picture yourself as doing beautifully whatever you seek to do.

5. While you work, concentrate in a constructive way on what you are doing. If you are painting a tree, think "tree"—think of the sturdy trunk rooted in the ground, drawing nourishment from the soil; think of the leaves that murmur in the breeze, that lift their faces to the sun, that glisten in the rain, that provide shade for the traveler. In a light-

hearted way be a bit poetical about it all, and you'll paint a better tree.

6. Keep your artist's materials in perfect condition and in order: your brushes clean and soft, your pencils well sharpened, varnish in perfect condition, tracing paper, linen, and frosted acetate smooth and free from wrinkles. Arrange things in an orderly manner, so that they are readily available for use.

7. Provide proper lighting when you work. A north window is best for daytime work. In the evening, you should have a lamp close by, directed right on your work.

8. Work in a clean room, and always dust the material or the article which you are ornamenting.

9. If a written instruction seems difficult to understand at first, read it aloud. Seeing an idea in print, and at the same time hearing it spoken (by yourself in this case) is often more effective than just seeing it alone.

21

Restoration of Old Decorated Pieces

Restoration requires a great deal of skill and experience, and therefore it should be undertaken only by one who has studied original pieces over a long period of time, and who has become an expert in the decorating techniques concerned.

Moreover, it must never be forgotten that most old pieces will be more highly esteemed when they have *not* been restored. Restoration, if not done by experts, can all too easily lessen the market value of an old piece. So the first rule in all cases must be to think carefully about the whole problem, and to act with the utmost restraint.

Other points to be considered are whether the decoration is genuinely old, and whether it has sufficient merit to justify restoration. Genuine worth-while decorations are recognized by their expert brushwork, their evidence of finely cut stencils, and their well-balanced, artistically conceived designs. As a rule, only the highly skilled decorator with many years of experience will be qualified to judge these points.

Although the following paragraphs give an outline of the procedures, each case must be studied to decide how much or how little work is required. Generally speaking, it is far better to do too little in the way of restoration rather than too much.

Cleaning

Remove surface dirt with the gentle and judicious application of a damp cloth and a little mild soap. Rinse with another damp cloth, and dry.

White Film

To remove any white stains or film caused by old shellac, use denatured alcohol on a cloth, but only a little at a time. Proceed cautiously, doing only a small section at a time, and if any color comes off, stop at once. A hint of white film may remain, but this will disappear when varnish is applied.

Removing Paint

If an old coat of paint covers an original decoration, the paint must be removed slowly and carefully to preserve the decoration. The repeated application of soap on a damp cloth is sometimes all that is needed. In some cases, rubbing small sections at a time with denatured alcohol will take off the paint. Or chipping off the paint bit by bit with a small knife may be best. In all cases, judgment and discretion must be exercised if the decoration is to be saved.

Note. Do not use the regular paint and varnish remover on an old piece. When dealing with an old piece that has been painted over, always proceed on the assumption that there is a decoration under the paint.

Removing Rust

In the case of tin objects, all rust must be removed. This may be done with Rusticide. Although this preparation will not harm paint, it should be applied just on the rust spots. A small paint brush is a convenient applicator. In rubbing with steel wool you should try to avoid as much as possible rubbing the paint and decoration surrounding the rusted area. Use steel wool twisted around a pointed stick. Rinse and dry.

Touching Up

Whenever it is at all possible, keep the original decoration, merely touching up background and decoration where parts are missing. Match colors as closely as possible. Bronze powders may be mixed with varnish on the newspaper palette, and applied with a small brush; if necessary, add touches of oil paint to get the color you want. After drying for twenty-four hours, the touched-up parts may be "antiqued," if need be, by using transparent overtones to match the original.

Complete Restoration

If too much of a decoration has disappeared to make touching-up feasible, make a careful copy of it on frosted acetate. The first step to-

[*102*]

ward this is to apply a coat of varnish and let it dry. The glossy surface will bring out more clearly all traces of the pattern. Make a careful tracing on the frosted acetate of everything that is even faintly visible. Sometimes all that remains of gold scrolls are faint impressions which may be seen when the painted surface is held at certain angles. Then put a fresh piece of frosted acetate over the tracing, and make a complete painted copy, supplying any missing sections from research or imagination. After this, you can proceed to remove the old finish entirely from the article, and start the job of restoration on the raw metal or bare wood.

Pitted Surface

After rust has been removed, or paint has been chipped off, the floor of an old tray may be badly pitted. In this case, take some thick sediment from the bottom of a can of flat black that has been standing awhile, and mix it with powdered pumice to make a heavy paste. Add a few drops of varnish, and use this compound as a filler, smoothing it on with a palette knife or your finger. Let this dry for several days, and then sandpaper it. For a colored background, use the appropriate color instead of flat black.

Gold Leaf Restoration

It is very difficult to match old gold leaf, but in cases where rust has set in, restoration is better than neglect. Make a tracing of the original pattern, and supply the missing parts. Transpose the outlines to the prepared surface. Then apply the gold leaf in the usual way over a mixture of Yellow Ochre and varnish. Let it dry for a week, and then apply a protective coat of varnish. When this is dry, use transparent colored overtones over the newly laid gold leaf to match as closely as possible the color of the old metal.

Restoring Old Painted Chests and Boxes

These pieces were usually painted and decorated with colors containing turpentine and linseed oil, and so require an oiling once a year to keep them in good condition. First, clean the surface by washing it carefully and gently. Wait twenty-four hours. Then treat the surface with a colorless or neutral lotion cream (such as is sold for fine leather shoes, handbags, etc.), applying it with a soft cloth.

If parts of the decoration need restoring, this should be done with

Japan and oil colors, mixed with turpentine, linseed oil, and a few drops of Japan Dryer to hasten the drying. Colors containing linseed oil require at least a week to dry thoroughly. This should be remembered when painting one color over another.

Avoid the use of Vermilion in matching mixed background colors. It never mixes properly with certain colors, separating after the mixed color has been applied and so changing that color.

Restoring a Stenciled Decoration

1. Trace the design on frosted acetate, accurately and precisely. Supply any missing parts.

2. Place architect's tracing linen over the acetate, and trace the missing parts. Cut the stencils.

3. Buy several shades of bronze powders corresponding as closely as possible to the colors in the original decoration.

4. Varnish the surface, and when it is tacky, stencil the missing parts. Let the work dry twenty-four hours.

5. "Antique" the newly stenciled parts, by mixing varnish with a touch of oil color, and applying a transparent overtone to match the original parts as closely as possible. Use as little varnish as you can, so that it will not form a ridge around the edges when it settles. When desirable, flatten or smooth out the edges of the varnish patch with the finger tip.

Another procedure is to give the area a coat of varnish; then, immediately wiping the brush almost dry, pick up minute bits of dry color on the brush, and go lightly over the newer parts until you get the color you want. If necessary, use a smaller brush to apply the color. This process requires great speed and considerable skill to get the color just where you want it and to avoid streakiness.

Portfolio of Additional Patterns

The patterns in the following pages are accompanied by brief directions for painting: the more detailed instructions can easily be found in the chapters on the various techniques. Students are advised to review those chapters, and to keep on practicing the brush strokes at every opportunity. Before each painting session, five or ten minutes of brush stroke practice is of inestimable value in improving your work and in saving time. Make perfect brush strokes your aim.

It is strongly recommended that you paint each of the patterns at least once on frosted acetate. This will give you practice in painting the various stages, in mixing colors, and generally in wielding the brush with facility. Many of my students take great pride in their painted patterns, which they mount carefully and keep in portfolios. This provides a convenient reference and a means of displaying the patterns to their friends.

Blue Dower Chest

Figures 17-20—Color Plate IX

The Frontispiece shows the general appearance of this splendid nineteenth century Pennsylvania painted dower chest which is preserved in the Metropolitan Museum of Art, New York. With its sunken arched panels and lovely tulip motifs the chest is of a type associated with Lancaster County. It measures 52 inches long, 26 inches deep, and 29 inches high.

In view of these dimensions, the line drawings in Figures 17-20 have naturally had to be reduced; but the outlines are simple, and enlargement to any other size you may require is not difficult (see Chapter 18). The original sizes of the parts are as follows: Figures 17 and 18—13½ inches high; Figure 19—13 inches high; Figure 20—15⅝ inches wide at the center line. The designs are painted on cream panels.

To make patterns on frosted acetate, first do any desired enlargement of the patterns in Figures 17-20. Make corrected tracings of the enlargements (see Chapter 18). Place frosted acetate over the tracings, and proceed in each case as follows.

Figure 17

1. In the three flowers marked V you see dotted areas on the petals: these indicate the Raw Umber that is to be worked into the wet color as you paint each petal. Work with two brushes: one, a showcard brush, with a dry mixture of Raw Umber; the other, a quill brush, with a mixture of salmon pink, made by mixing Vermilion, a little White, and a touch of Raw Umber. Using the quill brush, paint the petals one at a time with the pink, immediately working in a touch of the Raw Umber and blending it with the pink. Disregard all the superimposed details, and leave the large centers (in *all* the flowers) unpainted at this stage. With the same salmon pink, paint the petals of the flowers VM.

Mix Prussian Blue, a little White, Raw Umber, and a touch of Ja-

[*106*]

FIGURE 17   BLUE DOWER CHEST: CENTER FRONT PANEL

pan Vermilion, to make a dark medium blue, and paint the petals of the flowers B.

Mix some Yellow Ochre with a little Japan Yellow to make a golden mustard yellow, and paint all the flower centers. As you paint each center, work in on the wet surface the few strokes of dry Burnt Sienna which can be seen in the drawing. Allow twenty-four hours for drying.

2. Mix some Japan Green, a little Raw Umber, and a touch of Prussian Blue, to make a country green, and paint all the line-shaded parts as shown in Figure 17, disregarding the black strokes.

Mix some Yellow Ochre and Raw Umber to make a thin, somewhat transparent mixture of dark mustard yellow, and paint the flowers VM, going right over the salmon pink underpainting, but leaving hints of the salmon pink at the tips and here and there. Let dry twenty-four hours.

3. Mix Raw Umber and Prussian Blue to make a very dark blue, and paint the accent strokes shown as solid black in Figure 17. Then wipe the brush back and forth on the newspaper to flatten it and at the same time to get rid of most of the paint on it. With this, add the small, fine dry-brush sort of strokes on the petals of each flower.

Figure 18

This is painted in the same way as Figure 17, except that Figure 18 has no flower B.

The berries are in salmon pink.

Figure 19

The flowers marked V are in salmon pink. For the flowers O, mix some Japan Vermilion, a little Japan Yellow, and a little Raw Umber to make a dull orange. The oval and the heavy accents are painted in the same blue black color that has been used for the accenting strokes in the previous figures. The oval is best done with a striping brush. The line-shaded parts are painted as before (Figure 17).

Figure 20

This shows one half of the large oval which is centered on the lid of the chest. The centers of all the flowers are a purplish red, made by mixing Alizarin Crimson, Burnt Sienna, and a touch of Prussian Blue, and they are painted rather sloppily, with the mixture thicker and thin-

[*108*]

FIGURE 18   BLUE DOWER CHEST: FRONT PANE

FIGURE 19 BLUE DOWER CHEST: SIDE PANEL

CENTER LINE

Figure 20   blue dower chest: top panel

ner here and there. The petals of the flowers B are in the same blue as was used previously. The flowers VM are painted in two colors: first the dotted line parts are done in the salmon pink, and when this is dry (after twenty-four hours), the dull mustard yellow over-strokes are painted, each stroke partly obscuring the pink strokes.

There is no occasion to copy the old name on the lid, or to insert any name. But if you do happen to want to put a name on, do it in some old style of lettering.

To Decorate a Chest
1. Prepare the surface for paint (see Chapter 13).
2. Apply the blue background color.
3. Paint the recessed panels and the oval panels on top and sides of the chest with a cream color flat paint.
4. Apply the salmon pink trim.
5. Paint the decorations.

The Finish
Old ornamented chests were not originally painted with varnish in the colors, nor were the chests given finishing coats of varnish. If an old chest is to be restored, and needs just a little touching up here and there, mix your colors with turpentine and a little linseed oil, as the old decorators did. But to keep paint of that kind in good condition, it is necessary to rub it over once a year with neutral leather cream.

If, however, you are starting from the beginning on a chest, you will probably prefer to use varnish in mixing the colors, and to finish up with the six coats of varnish generally recommended. This finish wears better, and requires little or no attention.

Watering Can

Figure 21—Illustration 6

This pattern is done in freehand gold, with touches of light vermilion. To make a copy on frosted acetate, proceed as follows:

1. Cut a piece of tracing paper, 9 by 10 inches. Lay it over Figure 21, and make a complete tracing of the pattern, joining the two separate sections, (A) and (B), to the main pattern. Lay a piece of frosted acetate over your finished tracing.

2. With a thin mixture of Japan Vermilion and varnish, paint all those parts of the pattern shown in black in Figure 21, including the fine stems and grasses, but disregarding the white lines. When tacky, apply pale gold powder. Let dry twenty-four hours.

3. Remove all loose powder. Mix Japan Vermilion, Yellow Ochre, and a speck of White, to make a light vermilion, and paint the line-shaded areas in Figure 21. Let dry twenty-four hours.

4. With a quill brush and Japan Black, paint the black lines which in Figure 21 are shown in white.

The background color of the original watering can is black, and the striping is in gold.

■ PALE GOLD
VERMILION

FIGURE 21 WATERING CAN

ILLUSTRATION 6   TINWARE DECORATED IN GOLD LEAF AND GOLD BRONZE POWDER
Courtesy of Dr. and Mrs. Roswell P. Barnes

Seamed Coffin Tray

Figure 22—Illustration 6

From 1720 to 1830 British tinplate was imported for manufacture by our tinsmiths into household articles. As it came only in sheets 8 by 14 inches, many articles requiring larger sheets had to be pieced together. This tray, shown in Illustration 6, is an example. Such trays were usually decorated with a country pattern, and I rather think this one was re-decorated in the late nineteenth century with this gold pattern which has a distinctly Victorian air about it.

To make a copy on frosted acetate of this example of freehand bronze, proceed as follows:

1. Make a complete tracing of the pattern (section A, B, and C in Figure 22) on tracing paper, omitting the superimposed details on the leaves and flowers, which can be added later by eye. Place a piece of frosted acetate over your tracing.

2. With a thin mixture of Japan Vermilion and varnish, paint the whole pattern, referring to Illustration 6 as you work. When the work is tacky, apply the pale gold powder. Let dry twenty-four hours.

3. Remove all loose gold powder. With pen and ink, draw in the fine leaf veins and the details on the flowers, disregarding the dotted and line-shaded areas shown in section A of Figure 22. Wait half an hour for the ink to harden.

Mix a little Alizarin Crimson with a speck of Burnt Umber and enough varnish to make a light transparent red when applied to the gold, and paint the line-shaded areas in section A, immediately blending off the edges here and there with a clear varnish brush.

With a transparent Burnt Sienna, paint the dotted areas, blending off the edges here and there.

FIGURE 22   COFFIN TRAY AND BREAD TR

A

::: BURNT SIENNA
///// ALIZARIN CRIMSON

B

C

D

E

FLOOR BORDER   F

Red Foot Bath

Figure 23

To make a copy of this freehand bronze pattern on frosted acetate, proceed as follows:

1. Lay a piece of frosted acetate over Figure 23.

2. With a thin mixture of Japan Vermilion, paint the entire area of the building, trees, and foreground, disregarding all line details. Paint the area in sections. By this I mean that when you stop at any point in the process, you should stop along a line in the design—the line of the fence, or of the roof, or of the side of the building. Thus, when you resume painting there will be no unsightly hump made in a conspicuous place on the surface. When it is tacky, apply pale gold powder over the entire surface. The brush stroke borders around the top and bottom of the foot bath are also in gold. Let the work dry twenty-four hours.

3. Remove all loose powder. With pen and ink, add the line detail and shading.

The background color is an antique vermilion. The striping at top and bottom is in gold.

This pattern comes to us by courtesy of Mrs. Irene Lovett.

FIGURE 23 RED FOOT BATH

New York Table

Figures 24-27—Illustration 7

This pattern comes from a round table which was made about 1820, and is now owned by the Cooper Union Museum for the Arts of Decoration in New York City. It is made of "mahogany, stained to simulate rosewood," and the elegantly beautiful decorations are in gold leaf. The table, which is 30½ inches high and 35½ inches in diameter, is illustrated in Figure 24.

For practice purposes, make a pattern on frosted acetate, using pale gold powder instead of gold leaf. Proceed as follows:

1. Cut a piece of tracing paper 14 inches square. Fold it lengthwise and crosswise, open it up again and rule a line in pencil along each fold. This gives you the center of the paper, and this center you place on the center of the design in Figure 25. See that the ruled lines are over the lengthwise and crosswise center axes of the pattern. Holding the paper firmly in position, making a tracing of the main lines of the pattern, but omitting all small superimposed details that can be added later by eye. Shift the tracing in order to join the separate sections A and B to their proper places in the design. Then turn to Figure 26, and place the tracing over the C section given there, thus completing the whole design.

Similarly, make a tracing of the side design in Figure 26, connecting the separate sections to the main unit. Also, make tracings of sections F, G, and H in Figure 27.

2. Place frosted acetate over each of the tracings and proceed to paint the patterns in a thin mixture of Japan Vermilion, disregarding all pen line detail and shading. Keep looking at Illustration 7 for guidance. The star (H) is an outlined star, the center not being painted. As you paint, keep watching the parts already painted and apply the pale gold powder as they become tacky. Set the pattern aside to dry for twenty-four hours.

3. Remove all loose gold powder. With pen and ink, add the line detail and shading. The pen line work on the two center medalions of the two large designs is difficult to do by eye. So make a tracing of the

V   OLD COUNTRY TINWARE
Courtesy of the Society for the Preservation of New England Antiquities

VI   OLD "TINSEL" PICTURE
Courtesy of Miss Gertrude E. Robertson

VII NINETEENTH-CENTURY "FANCY" CHAIR
Courtesy of Mr. & Mrs. Vernon H. Brown

VIII JAPANNED RED SECRETARY, ENGLISH, C.1710
Courtesy of the Metropolitan Museum of Art

IX NINETEENTH-CENTURY PENNSYLVANIA PAINTED DOWER CHEST
Courtesy of the Metropolitan Museum of Art

main lines. Then put your gold pattern over a blotter or something equally soft, place the tracing on top of the pattern, and, with a sharp pencil, retrace the lines, making an indentation in the gold which can be followed with the pen. (Note that when doing a pattern on acetate it is not necessary to apply the protective coat of varnish preparatory to transferring the main pen lines). Complete the rest of the pen lines and the pen line shading. Allow the work to dry and harden for half an hour. This time is sufficient for a pattern—when decorating a table allow several hours for the pen lines to dry.

There is also quite a lot of transparent Burnt Umber shading on this pattern, but there is no practical way to indicate on the line drawings where this goes. So take a good look at Illustration 7, and you will see a lot of light gray shading, generally where the pen line shading is. This is the transparent Burnt Umber shading, and it is applied with a quill brush. Immediately after each stroke is made, the inner edges of the brown are blended off with a clear varnish brush. Sections F and G in Figure 27 are similarly shaded with transparent brown.

FIGURE 24   NEW YORK TABLE

FIGURE 25   NEW YORK TABLE: TOP

Figure 26   NEW YORK TABLE: TOP AND SIDES

a

b

F

G

H

TABLE TOP
BORDER

Figure 27   dressing table and new york table

ILLUSTRATION 7   GOLD LEAF DECORATION FROM A NEW YORK TABLE, EARLY NINE-
TEENTH CENTURY
Courtesy of the Cooper Union Museum

Dressing Table

Figures 27-29

This pattern comes from an old dressing table which is illustrated in Figure 28. When I first saw this table in an antique shop, it was of a dark-colored wood and the design was done in what appeared to be

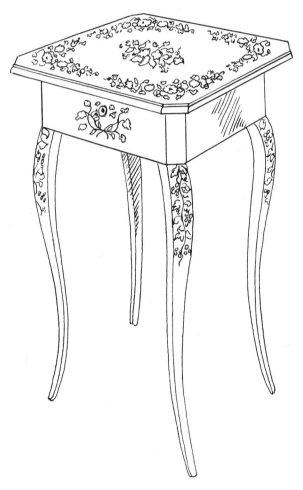

FIGURE 28   DRESSING TABLE

a gold leaf which had a particularly luminous quality. Closer inspection still left me wondering just what the "gold leaf" was. Some weeks later, on going back to the shop, I was dismayed to see that the many coats of varnish which had apparently covered the table had been removed, right down to the bare light-colored wood, at the same time revealing that the once gold-looking decoration was an inlay of thick white shell with finely etched detail. It was not nearly as attractive and impressive then as it had been before "restoration." But I feel justified in including this beautiful pattern here, and offer it as the gold leaf pattern it once seemed to be! It is adaptable to many purposes.

To make a practice copy of the pattern on frosted acetate in free-hand bronze, using pale gold powder, turn to Figure 29 and proceed as follows:

1. Make a complete tracing on tracing paper of the center spray, and of the corner spray, adding the separate part A to the corner spray at the place indicated. Disregard all penline superimposed details, which can be added later by eye. Place frosted acetate over your tracing.

2. With a thin mixture of Japan Vermilion, paint the pattern. Be sure to keep it all light and delicate, especially the fine stems. When it is tacky, apply palegold powder. Let the work dry twenty-four hours.

3. Remove all loose powder. With pen and ink, add the fine line details. Heavier black details can be painted in with a quill brush and Japan Black. Allow twenty-four hours for drying.

4. It greatly enhances the pattern to add touches of pale transparent Burnt Sienna shading, similar to those in the top spray in Figure 22. But in the present case I would confine the shading to just one color, the Burnt Sienna.

The keyhole spray, and the small vertical grape spray in Figure 27 are also part of this dressing table pattern, which is used here by the courtesy of Mrs. Irene Lovett.

Two Chair Patterns from Granville, Massachusetts:

Figures 30 and 31—Illustrations 8 and 9

Fancy chairs with stenciled decorations were being turned out in great quantities by 1820. Though made of common woods, many were painted and grained to resemble such more expensive woods as rosewood and walnut; others were painted a solid color, generally black. Lambert Hitchcock was the early chairmaker and stenciler whose name is best known to us to-day, and his factory was at what is now called Riverton, Conn. Another early chairmaker in Riverton was William Moore, Jr., who signed the chair from which the pattern in Figure 30 is taken. This chair is one of a set in the Granville, Massachusetts house of Dr. and Mrs. Louis Stevenson. The pattern which follows (Figure 31) is also from that Granville house, and although in this instance the chair is not signed, the testimony handed down in the family is that both sets of chairs were from the same craftsman.

When Moore worked alone he signed his chairs. Later, not growing too prosperous, he joined with Hitchcock, and they seem to have pooled their stencils, since chairs attributed to one of them display in many cases the same stencils as chairs attributed to the other. Moore was buried in Riverton, but his grave is unmarked. (The story goes that the gravestone was sold to pay for the mending of a crack in the church bell!)

First Granville Pattern (Figure 30. Illustration 8)

To make a copy of this pattern on black paper, proceed as follows:

1. Trace and cut the numbered stencil units shown in Figure 30, disregarding for the present the lettered units, these being a separate pattern. Notice that the leaf 3 has an arrow pointing to a curved line which represents the edge of the linen. This curved edge will be used as a guide in placing the veins in position on the leaf, as will be ex-

[*129*]

FIGURE 29   DRESSING TABLE

STILE

7 PALE GOLD

8 FIRE

9 PALE GOLD

6 PALE GOLD & FIRE

5 PALE GOLD

3 DEEP GOLD

4

1

PALE GOLD & FIRE 2

B

C

FIRE

PALE GOLD

A

plained in a moment. Incidentally, all the stencils of this pattern were used as a general illustration in Figure 4.

Number the units in ink to correspond with the numbers in Figure 30 and also write on each the bronze powders to be used. As is the case with all stencil patterns, you should practice the stenciling of this pattern on black paper until you can do it beautifully. Only then should any attempt be made to decorate an actual chair.

2. Cut a piece of tracing paper $12\frac{3}{4}$ by $4\frac{1}{2}$ inches, and make a layout tracing (see p. 40). Then cut a piece of black stenciling paper to the same size and shape as the layout tracing.

3. Varnish the black paper, and when this is tacky, turn to the photograph of the pattern (Illustration 8), and proceed to stencil. Place stencil 1 in position, checking the correctness of the position by holding your layout tracing just over it. Start by applying a little bright gold to the center highlight, then shading it off a bit with a little fire powder, letting it go quickly to black. Then add a little gold around the outer edge. Lift stencil 1, and place 2 in position, applying palegold to the brightest part, and shading off with fire to black. Add the barest hint of fire around the outer edge. Place 3 in position, stencil just around the edges with deep gold, shading off quickly to black. Stencil the leaf in its four positions around the peach. Then do the veins by placing the edge (4) of the linen in position and applying just a touch of powder for a vein. Move the linen along for each vein in turn: there are about seven veins in one leaf.

Next, put 5 in place, and stencil the two bright highlights first, fading off quickly to black, and then giving a suggestion of gold about the edges. The flower (6) is very bright palegold at the center, shading to fire, to black; then add a touch of gold around the outer edge of the flower. Next stencil 7 in palegold, followed by 8 in fire, leaving about half the berry black, on which you can add 9 in gold. Last of all, take 3 again and add it behind the strawberries, behind one of the fruits (5), and behind one of the flowers.

When all is complete, half close your eyes, and compare your pattern with the photograph for overall values. If your pattern is very much brighter, you will know you have used too much gold; and if your pattern is much darker, it will be obvious you have not used enough. Learn to evaluate your own work, and don't be too easily satisfied. Probably you will have to do the pattern two, three, or more times before you get just the right effect.

[*131*]

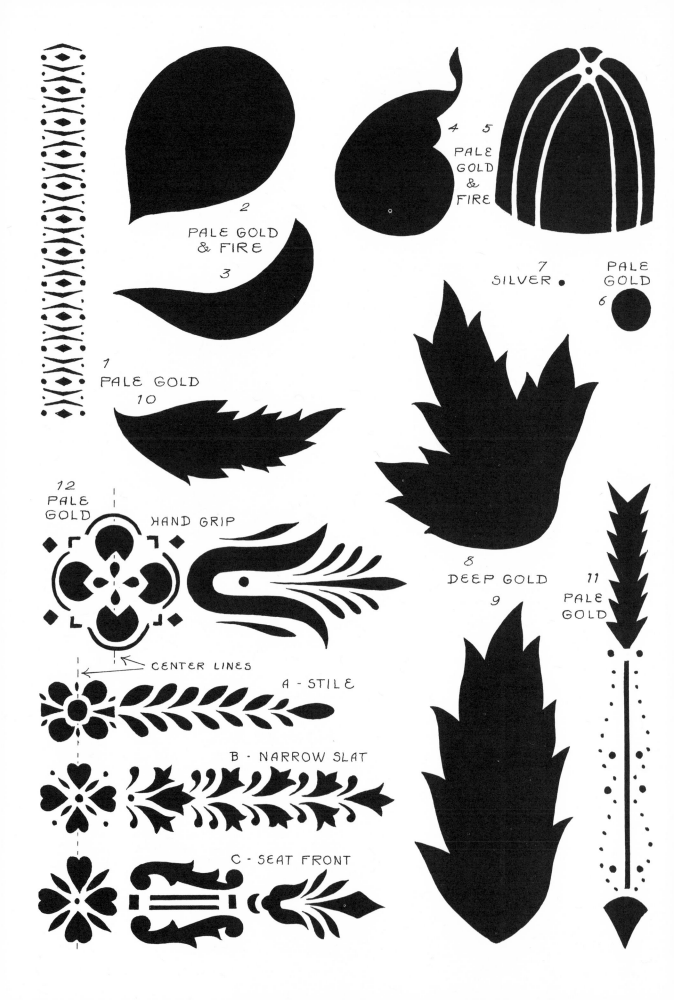

PALE GOLD & FIRE 2

PALE GOLD & FIRE 3

4 5 PALE GOLD & FIRE

7 SILVER .

PALE GOLD 6

1 PALE GOLD

10

8 DEEP GOLD

9

11 PALE GOLD

12 PALE GOLD

HAND GRIP

CENTER LINES

A - STILE

B - NARROW SLAT

C - SEAT FRONT

Second Granville Pattern (Figure 31—Illustration 9)

To make a pattern on black paper, proceed as follows:

1. Trace and cut the numbered stencil units in Figure 31, disregarding the lettered units (which are quite separate pieces not connected with the numbered ones). In tracing unit 12, note the center guide line, with one complete half of the unit on the right of it. Trace this half, and then turn the linen around and trace the other half.

Number the pieces in ink to correspond with the numbers in Figure 31, and also write on each the bronze powder which applies to it.

2. Cut a piece of tracing paper 12½ by 4 inches, and make a layout tracing. Then cut a piece of black paper in the same size and shape as the layout tracing.

3. Varnish the black paper, and when it is tacky, proceed to stencil, using Illustration 9 as a guide for shading. Stencil the pieces in their numerical order. Where palegold and fire are indicated, always use pale gold where the photograph shows the brightest parts to be, shading off to fire, and then to dark or black.

In stenciling the grapes (6), always stencil first the grape that is most to the front in the group of three, then add those behind. Always leave a large portion of each grape black, so as to give the impression of roundness. When all the grapes are stenciled, the silver highlight (7) is added. Place it in each case in the dark part of the grape.

Units 10 and 11 were taken from the stiles of this chair (see Illustration 15).

FIGURE 31   STENCILS FOR SECOND GRANVILLE CHAIR

ILLUSTRATION 8   FIRST CHAIR PATTERN FROM GRANVILLE, MASSACHUSETTS
Courtesy of Dr. and Mrs. Louis T. Stevenson

ILLUSTRATION 9   SECOND CHAIR PATTERN FROM GRANVILLE, MASSACHUSETTS
Courtesy of Dr. and Mrs. Louis T. Stevenson

[*134*]

Hitchcock-Type Chair Pattern

Figure 32—Illustration 10

To make a pattern on black paper, the proceeding is:

1. Trace and cut the stencils, noting that the linen of unit 2 has a curved edge numbered 3 which will be used as a guide in the placing of the leaf veins, as described on p. 129.

Number the units in ink to correspond with the numbers in Figure 32, and write on each the bronze powder to be used with it.

2. Cut a piece of tracing paper $13\frac{3}{8}$ by $5\frac{1}{4}$ inches, and make the layout tracing (see p. 33). Then cut a piece of black stenciling paper in the same size and shape as the layout tracing.

3. Varnish the black paper, and when this is tacky, proceed to stencil, using Illustration 10 as a guide for shading.

4. Begin with the border stencil (1), stenciling first on one side, then on the other. Then stencil the large leaf (2), followed by the veins (3). Next come the two melons (4), which are bright palegold at the top, shading into fire, and thence to black. Continue stenciling the units in the order of their numbers, completing the pattern for the slat with 14. Unit 15 is the top of the stile, and the other part of the stile is given in Figure 37. See Illustration 15 for the placing of these units on a chair stile.

This pattern comes from a chair owned by Mrs. C. Van Dorn Smith of Port Washington, Long Island.

1

2
PALE
GOLD

3

7
FIRE

6
PALE GOLD
5

8
PALE GOLD
& FIRE

4
PALE GOLD
& FIRE

9
PALE GOLD

11
PALE GOLD
10

13

12
PALE GOLD
14

15
TOP OF
STILE

HAND GRIP & SEAT FRONT

FIGURE 32   HITCHCOCK-TYPE CHAIR STENCILS

ILLUSTRATION 10   HITCHCOCK-TYPE CHAIR PATTERN
Courtesy of Mrs. C. Van Dorn Smith

ILLUSTRATION 11   TURTLE-BACK CHAIR PATTERN
Courtesy of the Cooper Union Museum

Stenciled Turtle-Back Chair

Figure 33—Illustration 11

Proceed as follows in making a copy on black paper of this pattern, which comes from a chair in the Cooper Union Museum, New York:

1. Trace and cut the stencil units in Figure 33. Make separate stencils for the veins of the leaves, to be applied as shown on leaf 12. Number the units in ink to correspond with the numbers in Figure 33.

2. Cut a piece of tracing paper 13 by 5½ inches, and make a layout tracing, using Illustration 11 as a guide. Then cut a piece of black stenciling paper to the same size and shape as the layout tracing.

3. Varnish the black paper, and when it is tacky, proceed to stencil, using Illustration 11 as a guide to shading. Stencil the units in their numerical order. When you stencil the bowl (3) fade off the upper right-hand corner to black, so that when you put leaf 4 in position, there will be black between it and the bowl; thus giving the leaf the appearance of overhanging the bowl.

In stenciling the fruit alongside the leaf, lay unit 5 in position, but before applying any gold powder, lay unit 6 right over it. In this position, stencil 6. Then lift 6 and stencil 5. In stenciling the grapes, stencil first those on the right side of the bowl; then clean the stencil on both sides with cleaning fluid, pat it dry, and, having turned it over, stencil the grapes on the other side of the bowl. The faint "clouding" on the bowl which can be seen in the photograph, is done last of all, that is, after all the units have been stenciled. Without using a stencil at all, and after waiting until the surface is almost completely dry, lightly add the gold "cloud," using *very* little powder on your velvet.

[*138*]

FIGURE 33   TURTLE-BACK CHAIR STENCI

ALL IN PALE GOLD
EXCEPT #12
WHICH IS IN
DEEP GOLD

STILE

DEEP GOLD

Stenciled Fruit Basket Chair

Figure 34 and 38—Illustration 12

To make a copy of this pattern on black paper, these are the steps.

1. Trace and cut the stencils, disregarding all line shading, both black and white. Note that the unit 12 has detail at the edge of the linen. (This combination is similar to the leaf stencil illustrated in Figure 4.) Number the units in ink to correspond with the numbers in Figure 34.

2. Cut a piece of tracing paper to size $12\frac{1}{2}$ by $4\frac{3}{8}$ inches, and make a layout tracing. Then cut a piece of black stenciling paper to the same size and shape as the layout tracing.

3. Varnish the black paper, and when it is tacky, proceed to stencil, using Illustration 12 as a guide for shading. In stenciling the basket (1), make it very bright palegold through the center, but not so bright toward the sides, so as to give the effect of roundness. Stencil 3 in palegold, brighter through the center, fading off a bit to the sides; then, after picking up all excess gold powder, life the stencil, and, with a clean part of the velvet, pick up the barest speck of fire powder and add the touch of fire "clouding," indicated by the line shading in Figure 34.

When stenciling the bunch of grapes, carefully observe the shading in the photograph. Also observe the shading in unit 12; a large area in the center being left black, on which 13 is placed and the bright gold touch added to the center.

The stencil for the stiles of this chair is at the bottom of Figure 38. The seat front and hand grip ornaments were completely worn off the chair, so others may be substituted.

The original chair from which the pattern is taken belongs to Miss Mary Aileen Dunne of Garden City, Long Island.

FIGURE 34   FRUIT BASKET CHAIR STENCILS

ALL IN PALE GOLD
EXCEPT SHADED
PARTS WHICH ARE
IN FIRE

(LINEN)

ILLUSTRATION 12 STENCILED FRUIT BASKET CHAIR PATTERN

Courtesy of Miss Mary Aileen Dunne

ILLUSTRATION 13 VARIOUS FURNITURE STENCILS

Boston Rocker

Figure 35 — Color Plate I

A copy of this pattern on black paper is made as follows:

1. Trace and cut the stencil units in Figure 35, but omit No. 1 for the time being. When you come to put this pattern on a rocker, you will probably have to alter that unit to adapt it to the ends of your slat. Meanwhile you can practice stenciling the main part of the pattern.

Number the units in ink to correspond with the numbers in Figure 35, and also write on each the bronze powders to be used.

2. Although the length of the entire slat is 23⅜ inches, cut a piece of tracing paper only 13 by 4¾ inches in order to make a layout tracing for the main center design. Use the color plate as a guide, and your cut stencils on Figure 35 to trace the units. The center design from leaf tip to leaf tip actually measures 11¾ inches, and the height is 4½ inches. Next cut a piece of black paper which may conveniently be the same size as the tracing paper.

3. Varnish the black paper, and when it is tacky, stencil the pieces in their numerical order, beginning with 2, which is brighter in the center, not so bright at the sides. The two large flowers (3) are done in silver-gold by picking up a tiny bit of gold on the velvet fingertip, and a tiny bit of silver at the same time. Refer to the color plate for the shading. Lift the stencil, and picking up a touch of fire powder on a clean part of the velvet, add the tiny "cloud" of red to the centers. Set aside to dry for twenty-four hours after all the pieces have been stenciled.

4. Remove all loose powder from the pattern. Study the color plate for the coloring.

The center portions of the two large flowers are given a wash of transparent red (Alizarin Crimson with a touch of Burnt Umber). The outer portions are a paler red, to which is added a touch of transparent green. To do this, mix a puddle of red with one quill brush, and a puddle of green with another. Paint the center portion of the flowers, excluding the dots; then, picking up a little extra varnish to make a paler red, paint the outer portions, immediately adding a touch of

2 PALE GOLD

4 PALE GOLD

3 SILVER-GOLD

5 PALE GOLD

6

7 FLOWER IN SILVER-GOLD

1 PALE GOLD

green here and there with the green brush. But the latter should have very little green on it, or the whole thing will flood out of bounds.

The cherries are given a touch of red, blended off with a clear varnish brush. The small flower is given a wash of transparent blue, and the leaves a transparent green.

This pattern is available through the courtesy of Mrs. Roderick Dhu MacAlpine of Doswell, Va., and of the owners of the original Boston Rocker, Mr. and Mrs. Carstairs Bracey of Bracey, Va.

FIGURE 35   BOSTON ROCKER STENCILS

Eagle Clock Pattern

Figure 36—Illustration 14

To make a copy of this pattern on black paper, proceed as follows:

1. Trace and cut the stencil units in Figure 36. The smaller dots in unit 14 can be punched with a hot needlepoint. Push a needle through a cork, and use the cork for a handle. Hold the needle with the point in a gas or other blue flame for a second or two; then punch two or three holes. Reheat the point and continue. When the holes are done, cut off any jagged edges of linen underneath, or lightly sandpaper them off with very fine sandpaper.

Number the pieces in ink to correspond with the numbers in the Figure, and also write on each the bronze powders to be used.

2. Cut a piece of tracing paper 13½ by 3¾ inches, and make a layout tracing of the eagle portion of the pattern, using the photograph as a guide. Cut a piece of black stenciling paper the same size and shape as the layout tracing. Also cut a piece of black paper 16½ by 2 inches for the pilaster design shown below the eagle portion.

3. Varnish the two pieces of black paper, and when these are tacky, proceed to stencil the units in their numerical order, keeping a careful watch on the photograph to get the proper shading, and using your layout tracing for the placing of the units.

The feather marks on the eagle's wings are done like shaded leaf veins, and for this purpose the X-edge on unit 4 is employed; but this time use deep gold powder. The same X-edge can be used for the leaf veins of leaf 9, but here silver powder is required. The eye of the eagle is done in pen and ink when the stenciling is dry.

Units 12, 13, 14, and 15 together comprise the design on the two upright pilasters of the clock, although the photo shows the pattern "lying down." Unit 12 is done in palegold, after which a little fire clouding is applied to the centers of the three flowers.

The source of this material is a shelf clock owned by Mr. Richard J. Metzger, Staten Island.

FIGURE 36 EAGLE CLOCK STENCIL

ILLUSTRATION 14   EAGLE CLOCK STENCIL PATTERN

Courtesy of Mr. Richard J. Metzger

ILLUSTRATION 15   VARIOUS FURNITURE STENCILS

Various Furniture Stencils

Figures 30, 31, 37, and 38—Illustrations 13 and 15

It is useful to have a few extra furniture stencils on hand to fill needs that may arise. Old stenciled chairs originally had designs on the stiles (the posts on either side of the chair back), on the seat fronts, on the hand grips, and sometimes on the narrow supplementary slats. But a number of the chair patterns illustrated in other figures do not have all their accessory designs because the latter became so worn on the original chairs that they could not be copied.

Figure 37 includes an extra stile and a seat front. Figure 38 shows two seat fronts from stenciled rockers, a narrow slat, and the stile pattern from the stenciled fruit basket chair. Also included in Figure 38 are three small border patterns of two units each. Each of these borders should be traced with its two units on one piece of linen, one inch apart, and with the usual inch margin all around. They are stenciled in the same way as the chair border on the rocker, directions for which are on p. 39. The star border and the leaf border come from an old piano, the brush stroke border from a wardrobe.

In Figure 30, sections A, B, C, and X comprise a chair slat pattern taken from an original stencil in the Metropolitan Museum of Art, New York. I suggest stenciling section A first in palegold, turning to Illustration 13 for the shading. Sections B and C might then be done in fire powder. This pattern is very suitable for a secondary slat in a two-slat chair.

The lower left-hand corner of Figure 31 shows separate units for a stile (A), a narrow chair slat (B), and a seat front (C). Note that these three are traced in the same way as unit 12, the directions for which are given on p. 133.

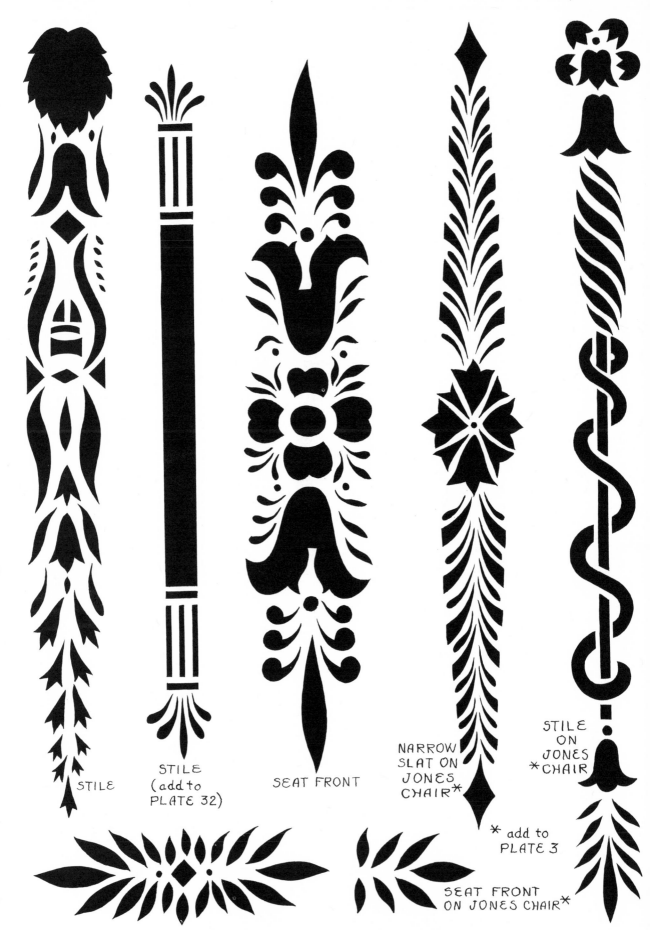

STILE

STILE
(add to
PLATE 32)

SEAT FRONT

NARROW
SLAT ON
JONES
CHAIR *

STILE
ON
JONES
* CHAIR

* add to
PLATE 3

SEAT FRONT
ON JONES CHAIR *

FIGURE 37 VARIOUS FURNITURE STENCILS

SEAT FRONT ON ROCKER

NARROW SLAT

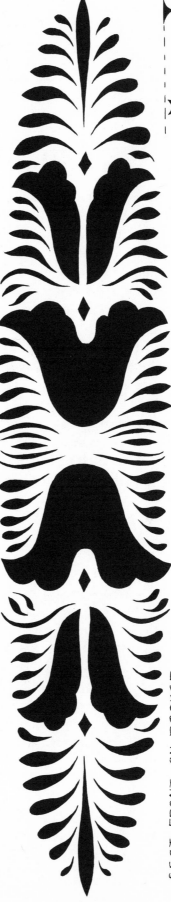

SEAT FRONT ON ROCKER

BORDERS

STILE

BORDER

FIGURE 38 VARIOUS FURNITURE STENCILS

The Stenciled Cornice

Figures 39-42 — Color Plate III

Many beautiful decorated curtain cornices, made about 1790 to 1810, are to be found in the larger and finer old houses, and in museums. Often the designs were stenciled, like the central part of the one shown in Color Plate III. This copy of the decoration on a cornice now in the Cooper Union Museum of Arts and Decoration, New York, was photographed for our present purposes because a photograph of the cornice itself does not bring out the pattern details clearly enough.

This pattern is a difficult one, and should not be attempted until you have had plenty of practice in doing all the other stencil patterns.

The basic color of the cornice is a dull olive green, and the border molding and other very bright gold parts seen in Color Plate III are in gold leaf. The stenciling is done in pale gold and fire bronze powders on an underpainting of black. The birds in the diamond-shaped side panels are in freehand bronze, also on a black underpainting.

It is suggested that the pattern on frosted acetate be done in sections, as the whole is too large for comfortable handling. The rectangular panel containing the main stenciled design is $33\frac{3}{8}$ by $4\frac{7}{8}$ inches, not including the border molding, which is $\frac{7}{16}$ inches wide. The overall dimensions of the cornice are 47 by 13 inches.

Turn to Figure 40. Trace on linen, and then cut out, the stencil units 2, 3, 4, and 5. Note that unit 4 consists of five small parts, all of which may be put on one piece of linen for convenience. Turn to Figure 41, and do the same with the units 1 to 10, and also the two large fruits in Figure 42. Number each unit in ink to correspond with the numbers in the figures, keeping those from Figure 40 in a separate envelope labelled "Basket Section." Also mark on each piece in ink the color of the bronze powder to be used.

From this point on I shall give the steps in decorating an actual cornice, but it should be understood that the stenciled sections and the birds and foliage must be practiced first on frosted acetate (*not* black stenciling paper).

[*152*]

FIGURE 39   CORNICE: BIRD AND FOLIAGE

PALE GOLD 2
& FIRE
3

LEAFY EDGE

LAYOUT

5

5

5

5

5

5

5

5

5

5

5

5

5

4 PALE GOLD

1 GOLD LEAF

PALE GOLD
5

FIGURE 41   CORNICE: STENCILS AND PARTIAL LAYOUT

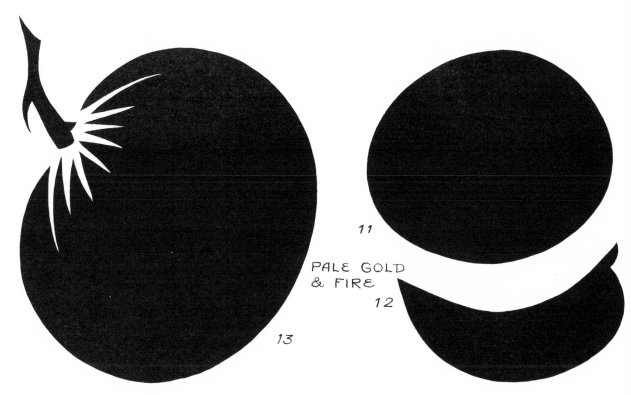

11

PALE GOLD
& FIRE

12

13

FIGURE 42   CORNICE: STENCILS

To decorate an actual cornice, proceed as follows:

1. Paint the whole cornice a dull olive green. Let it dry and harden about a month.

2. Make a tracing on tracing paper of the two sections containing leaves and flowers in Figure 39, altering them if necessary to fit your cornice; also a tracing of the basket outline (unit 1) in Figure 40. Transfer these outlines to the cornice. Then paint the areas and lay the gold leaf. Also lay gold leaf on the moldings and borders. Let this dry and thoroughly harden for a week.

3. Starting with the basket section, Figure 40, make a tracing of the outline of the area occupied by the fruits and leaves. Transfer this to the cornice. Paint the area with a thin, slightly transparent mixture of Japan Black, prepared beforehand in sufficient quantity for the job (use a very large bottle cap). Work quickly and smoothly, so covering the area that it will not be necessary to go back to touch up. The black mixture should be sufficiently thinned with varnish for it to dry with a smooth glossy black surface. Make a layout tracing.

[156]

When the surface is tacky, proceed to stencil the units in rotation. Where two powders are indicated in one unit, always use palegold for the brightest part, shade off quickly to fire, and finally to black. Use the color plate as a guide for shading, and your layout tracing for the placing of the stencils. The gold highlight dot doesn't show much, but it is there on the shadow side of each grape. Then add the palegold on the outer leafy edge, without using any stencil. Set it aside to dry.

4. For the main stenciled section on the long horizontal panel, cut a piece of tracing paper $33\frac{3}{8}$ by $4\frac{7}{8}$ inches. Now trace the "leafy edge" outline (Figure 41) two and three-quarters inches in from each end, reversing the tracing paper for the right hand side. Transfer these outlines to the cornice. Then, on the same tracing paper, continue to make a layout tracing for the pattern, beginning by tracing the upper part of Figure 41; and going on to complete the stencil units in Figures 41 and 42, all the time using the color plate as a guide. Take the time to do this carefully, which will make the actual stenciling much easier to do.

5. Using a thin mixture of Japan Black, begin with a large quill brush to paint the area on the cornice which is to be stenciled, starting with the leafy edge at one side; then, using a larger brush, such as a flat half-inch black bristle brush, lay the main area of paint as quickly and smoothly as possible; finish up with the quill again at the leafy edge at the other end. Work quickly and smoothly, so covering the area that it will not need any going back to touch up. Prepare a sufficient quantity of black mixture before you begin, so that it will not be necessary to stop in the middle of the painting to mix paint. It should dry with a smooth glossy black surface.

When the surface is tacky, begin stenciling with the small flowers and leaves at both ends, using units 1, 2, 3, 4, and 8. The palegold applied to the "leafy edge" is done without a stencil. Then stencil the large center flowers 5 and 6, all the time using the color plate as a guide to shading, and your layout tracing for placing the units. 5 and 6 are palegold at the center, shading to fire, and with fire around the edges, leaving the surface very dark where the vein lines (7) are to go. To speed up the stenciling and to avoid scratching the surface with your finger nails when you pick up the stencils from the tacky surface, use a palette knife to lift the stencils each time.

Go on to the small flowers above and below, and last of all do the large fruit units 11, 12 and 13. These are done when the surface has become fairly dry, thus enabling one to get that beautiful graduated shading, fading out so that the edges of the fruits are barely discernible. Last of all, add the leaf veins 9 and 10 which not only go on the leaf 8, but also are used here and there without the leaf by way of space fillers. Set aside to dry.

6. The birds in the diamond-shaped end panels are painted in thin Japan Black. When they are somewhat drier than the ordinary tacky stage, the palegold powder is added in the places where the fine line shading appears in Figure 39, toning off quickly to black. The brush strokes on the wings and tail, indicated in black in Figure 39, are done with a spit-brush and palegold powder. Take a small quill brush, moisten it with saliva, and then lay it lengthwise on a mount of loose palegold powder, thus picking up some of the powder. With this, paint in the brush strokes on the still tacky surface. Replenish the brush with saliva and gold powder as needed. (Keep a supply of saliva on your left forefinger to re-moisten the brush—don't get the gold powder in your mouth.) Set the work aside to dry for twenty-four hours.

7. When everything is thoroughly dry, remove every speck of loose powder from the cornice. Then add the black accents on the gold leaf leaves and flower (Figure 39), the detail on the basket (Figure 40), and the veins in the "leafy edge" Figures 40 and 41). Use pen and ink for the smaller and finer strokes if you like, but Japan Black and a quill brush for the heavier accents. Set aside to dry.

It should be noted that the black veins and leaf strokes in the "leafy edge" are seen in the drawing (Figures 40 and 41), but not in the color plate where, however, they ought also to be.

8. Do any necessary touching up with the olive green background paint or the Japan Black.

Country Tinware Patterns

The earliest American colonists naturally had to import all household articles of tinware. But as time went on, they bought tinplate from England, and local tinsmiths made it into the various articles which were in demand. The first known tinsmith in this country was Shem Drowne, who started work in Boston in 1720. It cannot have been long before others were at work in Philadelphia, New York, and the larger towns.

Around 1740 or 1750 (there is some question as to the exact date) Edward Pattison started the first large-scale manufacture of tinware at Berlin, Connecticut, and he conducted a flourishing business for many years. Candlesticks, candle molds, sconces, tea caddies, lanterns, canisters, trays, pie plates, boxes for all sorts of purposes, and many other household items were produced by him. A good many of them were decorated by local artists. Pattison's business flourished until the Revolution, and was resumed after the war. Among other centers where decorated tinware was prepared were Stevens Plains, Maine; Bloomfield, Connecticut; and Greenville, New York.

Tinware was not sold only in the localities where it was made. Larger enterprises sent out traders all along the Atlantic seaboard and west to the frontier towns. The Yankee tin peddler was a well-known character, and a welcome visitor to the early settlers, bringing essential products to them in the most out-of-the-way-places.

The following group of tinware patterns, consisting of a coffee pot, large canister, bread tray, syrup jug, and coffin tray, are taken from pieces owned by the Society for the Preservation of New England Antiquities, Boston. The Color Plate V shows some of these pieces. The greens have darkened with age, as they do so often, but the reds and yellows can be seen. Backgrounds for the designs were either dark asphaltum or black.

Coffee Pot (Figure 43)

1. Paint the four large "fruits" in Japan Vermilion, disregarding the superimposed details. Then mix some Japan Green with a tiny bit

of Raw Umber, and paint the areas shown in black. Wait twenty-four hours.

2. Mix a tiny bit of Burnt Umber with a lot of varnish to make a very thin transparent brown, and paint the line-shaded areas in the two lower "fruits." Don't fuss over this. Paint it and leave it; and be sure not to overload the brush. Use as few strokes as possible in the round centers. Wait twenty-four hours.

3. With a semi-transparent dark red, paint the dotted strokes. Wait twenty-four hours.

4. Mix some Japan Yellow with a little Raw Umber to make a mustard yellow, and paint the giant cross-hatching in the middle of the fruits. Each time you pick up a little mustard yellow with the quill brush, flatten the brush and paint with this flattened knife-edge, going back to the palette frequently to re-flatten the brush.

Add a little more Raw Umber to make a somewhat darker yellow, and enough varnish to give a hint of transparency, and paint the brush strokes shown by the fine cross-hatching in Figure 43. Wait twenty-four hours. This completes the pattern.

Large Canister (Figures 44 and 45)

Make a tracing of the complete design on a piece of tracing paper (omitting all details, which can be painted in later by eye), and mount it on white cardboard. Place frosted acetate over this, and proceed to paint.

Note, however, that the white half-band which is the background of the border design of leaves and berries (see Figures 45 and 15) need not be painted on the acetate. Make a note of it, and when decorating a canister remember to superimpose the off-white half-band after the main background color is completely dry, but before tracing the leaves and berries.

1. With Japan Vermilion, paint all the flowers, buds, and berries marked V. Mix Japan Green with a touch of Burnt Umber, and paint all the parts shown solid black in Figures 44 and 45. Wait twenty-four hours.

2. With a semi-transparent dark red, paint the dotted brush strokes on the vermilion parts.

Mix some Japan Yellow with some Burnt Umber to make a mustard yellow, and paint all the cross-hatched brush strokes. Wait twenty-four hours.

[*160*]

FIGURE 43 COUNTRY TINWARE: COFFEE P

LID

V   VERMILION
■   COUNTRY GREEN
▒   ALIZARIN CRIMSON
////   PALE BURNT UMBER
▨   MUSTARD YELLOW

FIGURE 44　COUNTRY TINWARE: CANISTER

V VERMILION
■ COUNTRY GREEN
※ ALIZARIN CRIMSON
//// THIN OFF-WHITE
※※ MUSTARD YELLOW
W OFF-WHITE BORDER

FIGURE 45   COUNTRY TINWARE: CANISTER

3. With a somewhat thin mixture of Japan Black, paint the leaf veins shown in the white (not dotted) lines in Figures 44 and 45.

With a semi-transparent off-white paint the line-shaded strokes on the flowers and buds, and the highlight strokes on the leaves shown in white dotted lines.

Syrup Jug (Figure 46)

1. Paint the large flower and the two buds in Japan Vermilion.

With a mixture of country green, paint the strokes shown in black. Wait twenty-four hours.

2. Paint the dotted brush strokes in semi-transparent dark red. Wait twenty-four hours.

3. With a semi-transparent off-white paint the line-shaded strokes.

Mix some Japan Yellow with a little Raw Umber to make a mustard yellow, and paint the cross-hatched strokes.

Bread Tray (Figure 46)

This is a border design on an off-white band, as can be seen in the Color Plate V. In decorating a bread tray, the off-white band should be painted after the background color is dry, but before tracing the design. First of all, hold a piece of tracing paper against one end panel of the bread tray, and carefully trace the outline of that area. Then place this tracing over the End Pattern on Figure 46, and draw the second curved line inward from the edge, to make the area of the off-white band. The band is slightly wider in the middle, and tapers off to the sides to meet the band on the sides of the tray. One tracing can be used for both ends of your tray. Make a similar tracing for one side of your tray, using the Side Pattern in Figure 46 as a guide.

Transfer this border area to the tray. Then paint in the off-white band, using a thin mixture of off-white to ensure a smooth surface. Let it dry at least twenty-four hours. Apply a second coat if necessary.

Put your tracings back over the patterns in Figure 46, and trace the leaves and berries, disregarding all details which can be painted in later by eye; and if necessary, adjusting the units to fit your border. Transfer the pattern to the off-white band on your tray, and proceed to paint the design.

1. Paint the berries in Japan Vermilion. Mix some Japan Green with a little Raw Umber, and paint the parts shown in black in Figure 46, but not the dots. Wait twenty-four hours.

[*164*]

FIGURE 46   COUNTRY TINWARE: SYRUP JUG AND BREAD TRAY

SYRUP JUG

LID

V   VERMILION
■   COUNTRY GREEN
▓   ALIZARIN CRIMSON
▨   THIN OFF-WHITE
▧   MUSTARD YELLOW
W   OFF-WHITE BORDER

W

V

W

END PATTERN

BREAD TRAY

SIDE PANEL

END PANEL

SIDE PATTERN

W

W

YELLOW BAND ON FLOOR

2. With a semi-transparent dark red, paint the dotted strokes.

Mix some Japan Yellow with some Raw Umber to make a rather dark mustard, and paint the floor border. Wait twenty-four hours.

3. Using a somewhat thin mixture of Japan Black, paint the leaf veins shown as dotted lines, and the black dots, on the ends and sides. Also paint the wavy line on the mustard floor border in black. Wait twenty-four hours.

4. Give the whole tray a coat of varnish. Wait twenty-four hours.

5. With Vermilion, and using a striping brush, stripe the edges of the broad white band with a thin stripe. Then mix some mustard yellow to match the floor border, and add the mustard stripe at the end and sides.

6. Finish the article in the usual way.

Coffin Tray (Figure 47)

This is another border pattern on an off-white band, and it is handled similarly to the bread tray pattern just described. The floor of the coffin tray is 11 by 7 inches.

1. Paint your tray black in the usual way.

2. The off-white band on the tray starts at the point where the floor meets the sloping flange. On a piece of tracing paper, trace the floor area of your tray, and then draw a second line one inch in from the first: the area in between takes the border. Measure the width of the border with a ruler on all sides, so as to be sure it is the same width all round. Transfer the second line to the tray, and paint in the off-white band. Let it dry thoroughly.

3. Put your tracing back on to Figure 47, and trace the border motifs, disregarding all details that can be painted in later by eye. If your tray differs in size and shape, you may have to adjust the design to fit. Transfer the design to the white border on your tray.

4. With Japan Vermilion, paint the berries. Wait twenty-four hours.

5. With a mixture of country green, paint all the parts shown in black. With a mixture of Japan Yellow and a touch of Burnt Umber, paint the tiny dots shown in outline on the berries. Wait twenty-four hours.

6. With a rather thin Japan Black, paint the veins in the leaves. Wait twenty-four hours.

7. Give the tray a coat of varnish. Wait twenty-four hours.

8. With a striping brush, paint the vermilion and mustard yellow stripes, as shown in Figure 47. Wait twenty-four hours.

9. Finish the tray in the usual way.

V   VERMILION
■   COUNTRY GREEN
///   ALIZARIN CRIMSON
W   OFF-WHITE BORDER
❊   THIN OFF-WHITE HIGHLIGTS

YELLOW
STRIPES

FINE YELLOW STRIPES
VERMILION STRIPE

Strawberry Box

Figure 47

A round cedarwood box, owned by Mrs. Vernon H. Brown, provides us with this pattern, the steps in painting which are as follows.

1. Paint the berries with Japan Vermilion. Wait twenty-four hours.

2. Mix some Alizarin Crimson and a touch of Burnt Umber to make a dark semi-transparent red, and paint one side of the berries, as shown by the line shading in Figure 47, blending off the inner edge of the red with a varnish brush. Wait twenty-four hours.

3. For the leaves and stems which are shown in black (but not for the curlicues), mix some Japan Green and a touch of Raw Umber to make a country green; with another brush, mix a lighter, yellower green by combining Japan Green, Raw Umber, and a little Japan Yellow. Deal with the leaves one at a time by painting each leaf in the darker green, and then with another brush immediately working in a little of the lighter green on the white-dotted areas which can be seen in the drawing to one side of each leaf. Wait twenty-four hours.

4. With Japan Black, paint the veins of the leaves, and the dots on the darker side of the berries. With some semi-transparent off-white, add the highlight on the berries, and on the turned-over edge of the one leaf, as shown by cross-hatching in the drawing. Wait twenty-four hours.

5. Mix some Japan Yellow and Burnt Sienna to make a warm mustard-yellow, and paint the curlicues and the dots on the lighter side of each berry.

FIGURE 47 WOODEN STRAWBERRY BOX, AND COUNTRY TIN COFFIN TRAY

Japanned Highboy

Figures 48-55—Illustration 16

Japanning has been called "the art of covering bodies by grounds of opaque colors in varnish which may then be either decorated by painting or gilding, or left in a plain state" (Robert Dossie, *Handmaid to the Arts,* 1764). It was devised as a means of imitating the beautiful and costly lacquered ware that was imported from the Orient, and which was so much admired in Europe and America.

The japanned highboy from which the patterns in Figures 48-55 have been taken is in the Metropolitan Museum of Art, New York. This handsome piece, made about 1700 of maple and pine, originated in New England, but shows the unmistakable influence of the East in its decoration.

If you compare the drawings in the line plates with the photograph, you will notice that some parts of the patterns stand out very clearly in the photograph, while others cannot be seen at all or only faintly. Use a magnifying glass to study the photograph. The parts that stand out were done in gold leaf over gesso, and comprise the important or story-telling parts of the decoration. Some of these important parts are darker than the others, and these were probably given a wash or overtone of transparent Burnt Umber in some cases, and of Burnt Sienna in others. The parts that are nearly or entirely invisible were probably done in a dark gold bronze powder. All the decorations show much wear, and are so darkened and cracked that it is difficult in some places to decide exactly how they were done. As a matter of fact, the photograph, for technical reasons, shows the decorations as much brighter than they appear to the eye in the actual piece.

Tracings

In doing a pattern of this type, the tracings of the various parts, as well as the acetate copies, are best done separately. Then, when you come to decorate a piece of furniture of your own, you can try out various arrangements with the minimum of effort. In this connection,

[*170*]

ILLUSTRATION 16   NEW ENGLAND JAPANNED HIGHBOY, C.1700
Courtesy of The Metropolitan Museum of Art

the boy leading the camel (Figures 53 and 54) is obviously one unit, and should be together on one tracing. Also the complete flower spray in Figure 52 should be on one tracing and in proper position, as shown in the small layout sketch. And the tip of the bird's tail in Figure 50 should be connected to the bird.

The corner decoration in Figure 54 is a sample of the supplementary or "fill-in" bits at the bottoms of the drawers. These were very crudely drawn and consist mostly of similar leaves and wiggly lines. It would not be worthwhile to use the space that would be required to show them all: you can easily supply your own if you need this type of "fill-in."

Patterns on Frosted Acetate

In making your acetate copies, use palegold powder for the gold leaf parts, referring always to the photograph. For the rest, use a deep gold powder, one that is much darker, so that there will be a strong contrast. In painting all stems, grasses, fine leaves, and trees, keep your work light and delicate. In painting figures, do the complete figure including the faces and hands. Later the flesh color will be painted over the gold. The superimposed details on the figures, flowers, leaves, animals, birds, buildings, vases, and other objects shown in penline in Figures 48-55 are painted in dark Burnt Umber over the gold, with a fine brush. For the detail on the camel's pack, use overtones of Burnt Umber, Burnt Sienna, and Raw Umber for contrast between the various parts.

The faces and hands were painted, but are so discolored by age that it is impossible to be sure what the original color was. I suggest mixing White, Alizarin Crimson, and Yellow Lake to make an Asiatic flesh color, subsequently adding enough varnish to make a rather thin mixture, and painting this over the gold. When this is dry, the features are detailed in dark Burnt Umber with a fine pointed brush.

Decorating a Highboy or Chest-of-Drawers

When decorating a piece of this nature, I like to put aside a room just for the purpose, where the piece can be laid on its back on the floor.

Although the background of the original was probably black, it has faded into an antique black, so if you want a really old effect, use a background of antique black (see p. 81). Assuming the black background has been properly prepared and is ready for decoration, the first step is to lay the various pieces of the finished acetate copies of the pattern in position on the upturned drawers, rearranging them as neces-

[*172*]

Figure 48   japanned high

TOP RIGHT HAND DRAWER

TOP LEFT HAND DRAWER

TOP LEFT HAND DRAWER

SECOND DRAWER

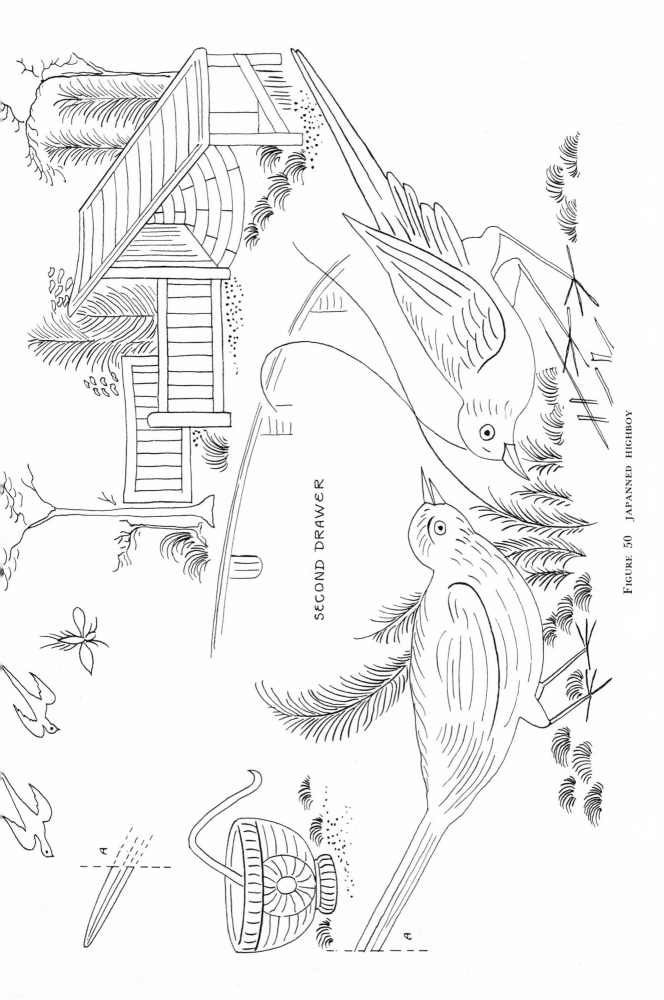

SECOND DRAWER

FIGURE 50   JAPANNED HIGHBOY

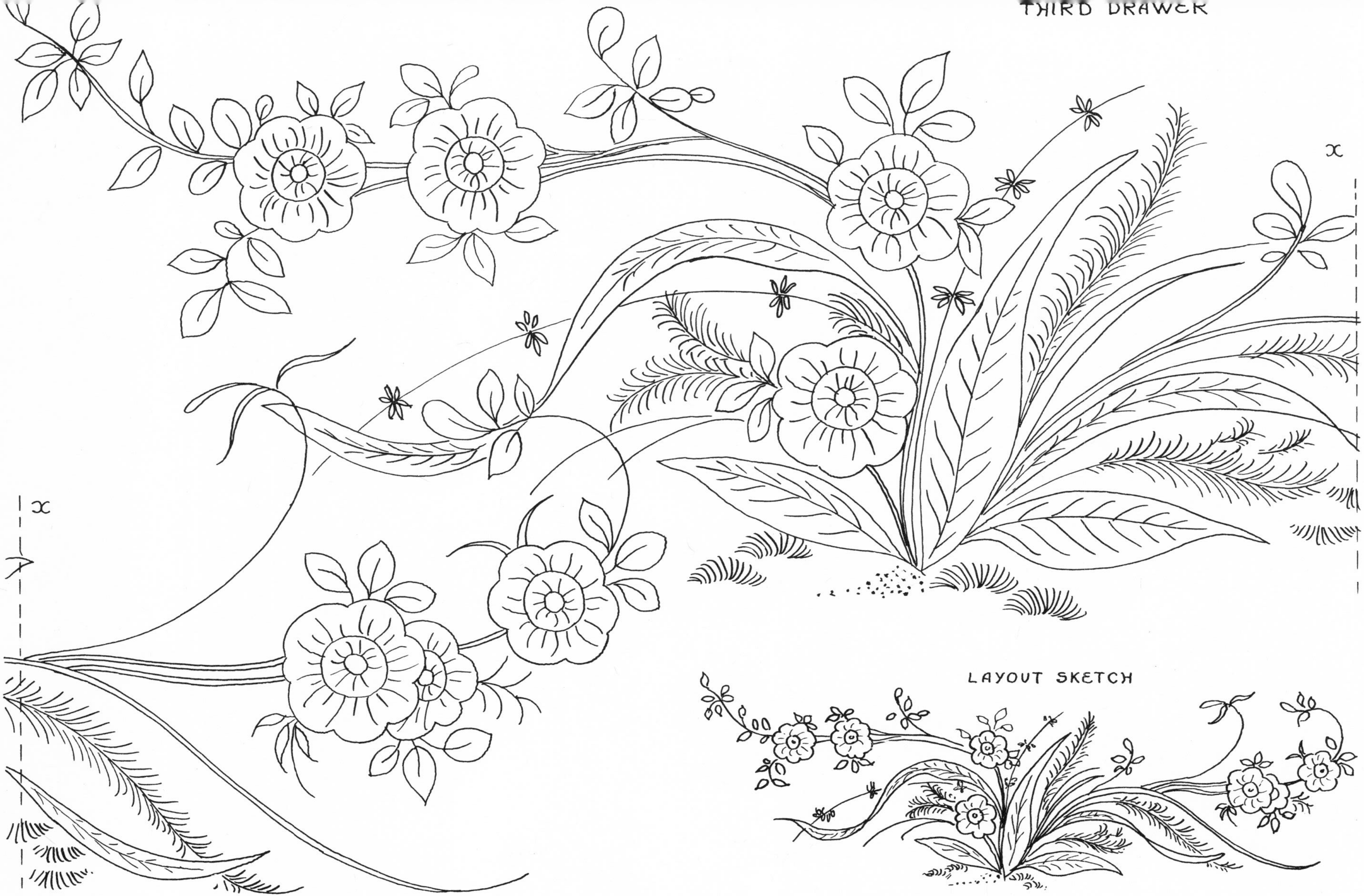
THIRD DRAWER
x
x
LAYOUT SKETCH

Figure 52 JAPANNED HIGHBOY

FOURTH DRAWER

LOWER LEFT HAND DRAWER

FIGURE 53 JAPANNED HIGHBOY

CORNER
DECORATION

LOWER RIGHT
HAND DRAWER

FOURTH DRAWER

FIGURE 54   JAPANNED HIGHBOY

FOURTH DRAWER

sary. Stand off to get the effect as a whole, adding extra birds, or leaves, or trees if and where needed. First consider the placing of the gold leaf parts only; then, when these are in their proper places, consider the supplementary or dark gold powder parts.

Transferring the Outline

Substitute the pencil tracings for the frosted acetate patterns, and trace the outlines of the gold leaf parts—and only the gold leaf parts: the outlines for the dark gold powder sections are traced later when you are ready to paint them.

The gold leaf parts of the design may be done over gesso (see Chapter 10) as on the original highboy, or they may be done without the gesso. The latter is just as beautiful, and, of course, requires a great deal less work. If you are not using gesso, don't forget to use whiting powder before transferring outlines.

Striping

The broad stripe around the edge of the drawers is in gold leaf. The narrow stripe inside the gold stripe is in dark gold powder.

FIGURE 55   JAPANNED HIGHBOY

Yellow "Fancy" Chair

Figure 56 — Color Plates II, VII

For a pattern of this chair on frosted acetate, the steps required are:

1. Cut a piece of tracing paper 20 by 4 inches, and make an outline tracing of the complete slat, disregarding all superimposed details, for these can be added later by eye. Place this tracing over a white cardboard, and put a piece of frosted acetate on top. Also, trace on linen and cut one grape stencil.

2. With a thin mixture of Japan Black (add enough varnish for the black to become slightly transparent and to dry, when painted, with a glossy surface), paint the center group of fruit and two large leaves, and the group of three brush strokes marked X.

Also with a thin mixture, this time of olive green (Japan Green and Burnt Sienna) paint the two end scrolls.

When the proper tacky stage has been reached, stencil the bunch of grapes in silver powder. Before adding the bronze shading on the other fruits and the leaves of the central design, wait half an hour or an hour longer, until the surface becomes very much drier and you think it's too dry. Then apply the pale gold and fire powders as shown in the color photo. Apply *very* little at a time, starting with the brightest parts, and shading off to black; leaving a good deal of the black showing. When the end scrolls also reach that very dry stage (which will take even longer because the mixture contained artist oil color), apply the pale gold, leaving a good deal of green showing. Disregard the brown strokes which are added later over the pale gold. Let the work dry twenty-four hours.

3. Remove all loose gold powder. Look again at the color photo. Mix some olive country green and paint all the green brush strokes around the fruit and leaves.

With a thin transparent mixture of Burnt Sienna, add the brush strokes on the end scrolls, blending off the edges here and there with a clear varnish brush.

[*182*]

END SCROLL →
→

TRANSPARENT GRAY
OLIVE GREEN
BURNT SIENNA
■ BLACK

FIGURE 56 YELLOW "FANCY" CHAIR

With a very thin, very transparent black, paint the broad band above and below the fruit and leaves, as indicated by the line shading in Figure 56. Set aside to dry twenty-four hours.

4. Add the black accents, the leaf veins, and the fine black stripe at top and bottom of slat. Use pen and ink for small, fine details, and quill brush and Japan Black for the larger, heavier details. This completes the pattern.

As regards the original, it is on a chair owned by Mr. and Mrs. Vernon H. Brown of New York. The background color is an antique pale yellow. The design on the seat front is similar to that in Figure 57, except that the leaves are pointed rather than rounded; and the thin gray strokes are in olive green. Striping on the chair is in black and transparent gray.

Pennsylvania Chair

Figure 57—Illustration 17—Color Plate II

Of the three sections in Figure 57, A and B were taken from the early nineteenth century Pennsylvania side chair (owned by the New York Historical Society) which is shown in Illustration 17. The main decoration is done in freehand shaded bronze with country brush strokes. See Color Plate II for the pattern of the top slat.

Although the background color of this chair, as it is today, appears to be a very pale yellow with a slight greenish cast, I rather think that originally it was an off-white. If I were decorating a chair with this pattern, I would start with off-white (with very little Raw Umber in the white), and count on the six finishing coats of varnish to give it a yellowish color. To achieve the slight greenish appearance, I would "antique" the first finishing coat of varnish by adding a touch of Raw Umber and the barest touch of blue to the varnish. But I would not advise attempting the blue unless you are quite an experienced decorator.

Section C in Figure 57 is from another chair, though of the same type, owned by the same Society. Both chairs, it is of interest to mention, originally belonged to a Reverend Samuel Jones, born 1737 and died 1811.

To make a copy on frosted acetate of all three patterns, proceed as follows:

1. Cut a piece of tracing paper 14 by 8 inches, and make an outline tracing of all three patterns, rejoining the separated sections D and E to the A design. Put a piece of frosted acetate over your tracing. Review the directions given for the Yellow Fancy Chair pattern on p. 182.

2. With thin Japan Black, paint all parts of the patterns that are neither dotted nor line-shaded in Figure 57. Keep looking at the color plate from time to time as you work.

When the surface has become almost dry, apply the silver, pale gold, and fire bronze powders, leaving plenty of black showing, as in the color plate. Let the work dry twenty-four hours.

3. Remove all loose powder. Then mix Japan Green, Raw Umber,

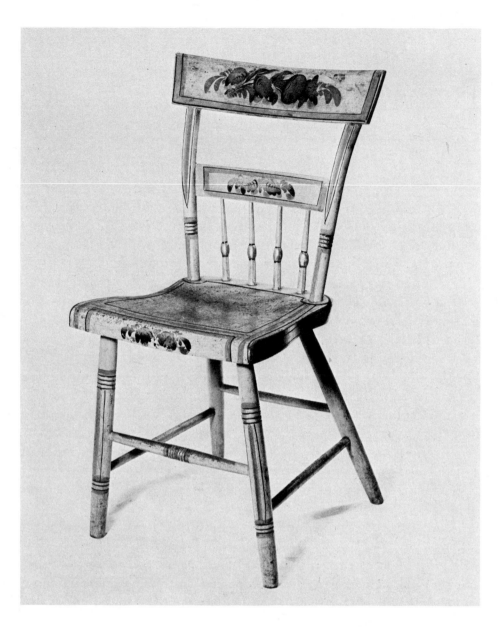

ILLUSTRATION 17   PENNSYLVANIA CHAIR, EARLY NINETEENTH CENTURY
Courtesy of The New York Historical Society

SEAT FRONT

A

B

C

D

E

COUNTRY GREEN
TRANSPARENT GRAY
BLACK

Figure 57 PENNSYLVANIA CHAIR

a touch of Japan Yellow, and a little white, making a yellowish light country green, and paint all the dotted brush strokes in Figure 57. If you were decorating a chair, you would at this stage also paint the broad green band as seen in the color plate, but you would add a little more varnish to the mixture so as to get a hint of transparency in the green of the band. Let the work dry twenty-four hours.

4. Mix a little Japan Black with a lot of varnish to make a transparent gray. Try the color out on a scrap piece of acetate to see if it is the same as in the color plate. Be sure not to have too much mixture on your brush or it will flood all over the place when you come to paint the pattern. If the color is not right, add more black or more varnish as the case may be. When the mixture is right, paint all the line-shaded parts in Figure 57. Allow twenty-four hours for drying.

5. Add the black veins and other details.

To Decorate a Chair

1. Apply the off-white background coats of paint.

2. Give the knobs of the spindles and the turnings of the upper part of the chair, a covering of the same pale gold lining powder that is to be used in the pattern. This is done by painting them with a thin mixture of varnish and Japan Black, and, when the surface is tacky, applying the gold powder. Let these dry twenty-four hours. Remove all loose powder.

3. Apply the decoration.

4. Varnish the whole chair in order to get a glossy surface for the striping. Allow twenty-four hours for drying.

5. With a thin, semi-transparent mixture of the same color green you used on the main slat, paint the broad stripes as shown in Illustration 17. Use a large striping brush. Dry for twenty-four hours.

6. Add the fine black striping (using Japan Black) as shown in Illustration 17.

Cheese Boat

Figure 58—Illustration 18

This pattern, which is done chiefly in gold leaf and freehand bronze, with some touches of stenciling, comes from a cheese boat owned by the Society for the Preservation of New England Antiquities, Boston. Section X of Figure 58 is a continuation of section B which is one of the long sides of the cheese boat, section A being the other. Section C was used on the semi-tubular ends.

The very fine leaf veins and the tiny twigs are in gold leaf, and for this kind of work it is best to use the gold-coated sheets of thin plastic sold by stationers for signing one's name in gold.

To make a pattern, proceed as follows.

1. With a mixture of Yellow Ochre and varnish, paint the areas shown in solid black in Figure 58. When the areas are tacky, lay the gold leaf as described in Chapter 9. Wait twenty-four hours.

2. Cut stencils for the four small shapes 1, 2, 3, and 4 at the lower right-hand corner of Figure 58.

3. With a thin mixture of Japan Black, paint all the remaining parts of the pattern with the exception of the tiny twigs, the flower stamens, and the butterflies' legs and feelers. When the tacky stage is reached, stencil the bodies of the butterflies with pale gold powder, using stencils 3 and 4; the suggestion of the dividing outlines of their wings by using stencil 1; and the turned-over leaf edges (all indicated by line-shading in Figure 58) by using stencil 2.

Wait another thirty minutes or so for the black surface to get still drier, and, using the palegold powder very sparingly, add the faint freehand touches of palegold indicated by the dotted areas in Figure 58 (no stencils used for this), at the same time adding touches of fire powder in the flowers and butterflies, and here and there on the stems. Leave plenty of black surface showing so that you get the overall dark effect as shown in the photograph. Wait twenty-four hours.

4. Make a pencil tracing of the fine leaf veins and twigs, the stems of the stamens, and the butterflies' legs and feelers. Place in position

■ GOLD LEAF
//// PALE GOLD STENCILING

C

B

A

x

x

STENCILS

1 2 3 4

over the painted pattern and secure the tracing at one end with bits of masking tape. Slip the gold plastic sheet, gold side down, between your tracing and the painted pattern. With a sharp hard pencil, retrace the lines.

With a camel hair quill brush dipped in varnish, go over the fine gold lines, and let this dry for twenty-four hours. The gold lines will thus be protected when you do the finishing coats of varnish.

5. With a mixture of varnish and deep gold powder, paint the stamen heads.

Paint the details in the butterflies' wings with Burnt Umber.

When you put this decoration on an actual cheese boat similar to the one illustrated, note that the striping on the long sides is done in gold leaf, as also are the "domes." This, of course, should be done at the same time as the gold leaf parts of the pattern.

FIGURE 58   CHEESE BOAT PATTERN

Guilford Blanket Chest

Figures 59 and 60—Illustration 19

This pattern is taken from an early eighteenth century painted pine blanket chest which originated in Guilford, Connecticut. It is painted in vermilion, off-white, and black on a brown stained background. The chest measures 46 inches long, 34 inches wide, and 19 inches deep. The main pattern (Figure 59) is 15 inches high in the original; the drawer pattern (Figure 60) is 7¼ inches high; and the tree on the sides of the chest is 19½ inches high. The background for this pattern might equally well be a painted brown one.

In painting the pattern, do the off-white parts first (see Illustration 19). The vase should be painted all in off-white, the decorative details in vermilion and black being done at a later stage. Use a striping brush for the long thin stems.

When the off-white parts are perfectly dry, paint the black parts, and last of all the red, which is Japan Vermilion mixed with a touch of Burnt Umber. The original chest has no striping.

CENTER

VERMILION
BLACK
OFF-WHITE

FIGURE 59 GUILFORD BLANKET CHEST

CENTER

TREE FOR SIDES OF CHEST

A

▨ VERMILION
■ BLACK
☐ OFF-WHITE

DESIGN ON DRAWER

FIGURE 60 GUILFORD BLANKET CHEST

ILLUSTRATION 18   CHEESE BOAT

Courtesy of the Society for the Preservation
of New England Antiquities

ILLUSTRATION 19   PAINTED PINE BLANKET CHEST FROM GUILFORD, CONNECTICUT,
EARLY EIGHTEENTH CENTURY
Courtesy of The Metropolitan Museum of Art

Index

A number in italics indicates an illustrated page.